in
other
words

a school thesaurus

by Patrick McLaughlin
with Iseabail Macleod

Schofield & Sims Ltd Huddersfield England

First Printed 1996
Reprinted 1998

In Other Words Exercises

ISBN 0 7217 0722 X

A separate book of exercises, based on **In Other Words**,
aims to give the pupils practice in the use of a thesaurus
and to develop their vocabulary.

Design and typesetting by Armitage Typo/Graphics Ltd,
Huddersfield

Printed in England by Ebenezer Baylis, Worcester

Introduction

In Other Words has been prepared especially for the needs of young learners and has two main aims: firstly, to give young learners a sense of the enormous variety of words, almost no two of which are exactly alike; secondly, to stretch and enrich their vocabulary. Learning a new word means we can express ourselves more precisely.

The headwords are based on vocabulary that young learners are already likely to possess. Each headword is followed by a list of words with similar meaning. These alternatives include words which may as yet be unfamiliar to the learner.

What is a thesaurus?

A thesaurus is not a dictionary. It does not give the meanings of words. Instead, it is a huge 'catalogue of words' arranged under topics or headwords, providing the reader with words which are similar in meaning to the headword.

Think about the colour charts you get from a paint shop. Under yellow, for example, you may see a dozen different shades ranging from nearly white to almost orange, but they are all 'yellow'. When choosing a colour to match the other colours in a room, you study all these different yellows before selecting the one you want.

It's the same with a thesaurus. You know roughly the word you are looking for, so you look under the relevant topic to find the right shade of meaning to suit what you want to write or say.

How to use this book

In a traditional thesaurus, words are arranged as ideas or concepts – for example, 'cold', 'heat', 'liking', etc. This can be difficult for a young learner to negotiate. Therefore, the words in this thesaurus are set out alphabetically, to make it more 'learner-friendly'. The suggested alternatives which follow the headword are also arranged alphabetically. Phrases are included in the alphabetical place of their initial letter.

Sometimes a word not only has shades of meaning but distinctly different meanings. For example, 'odd' can mean 'not even', 'unmatched', but it can also mean 'different' or 'strange'. These separate meanings are clearly numbered as 1, 2, 3, etc., and are arranged in their commonest order of usage.

Where appropriate, **opposites** are given (in green). Where words have different numbered meanings, the opposites are listed under the relevant meaning.

Each headword is identified as a **part of speech**, given in italics – e.g. **affair** *noun*. When a headword involves more than one part of speech, the usual order is *noun*, *verb*, *adj* and *adv*. This order is adhered to except where common sense or usage dictates otherwise.

A

taken **aback**	*adj*	amazed, astonished, astounded, shocked, surprised
abandon	*verb*	drop, forsake, give up, leave, leave behind, scrap
		opposites: continue with, persist in, support
abbreviation	*noun*	contraction, reduction, shortening, summary
		opposites: expansion, extension
abide	*verb*	accept, bear, endure, put up with, stand, tolerate
abide by	*verb*	agree to, carry out, comply with, go along with, keep to, stand by
ability	*noun*	capacity, competence, dexterity, expertise, gift, knack, proficiency, skill, talent
		opposites: inability, incompetence
able	*adj*	accomplished, capable, clever, competent, efficient, skilful, skilled, talented
		opposites: incapable, incompetent, weak
abnormal	*adj*	bizarre, curious, extraordinary, irregular, odd, peculiar, queer, strange, uncanny, unnatural, unusual, weird
		opposites: normal, regular, usual
abolish	*verb*	blot out, cancel, destroy, do away with, end, exterminate, get rid of, obliterate, put an end to, stamp out, wipe out
		opposites: continue with, keep going, preserve, retain
above-board	*adj*	above suspicion, forthright, frank, honest, on the level, open, straight, straightforward, trustworthy, truthful
		opposites: devious, dishonest, untrustworthy
abroad	*adv*	far away, in or into a foreign country, out of the country, overseas

abrupt	*adj*	1 hasty, irregular, quick, sudden, surprising, unexpected *opposites:* regular, slow, smooth
		2 brusque, curt, discourteous, impolite, rude, snappy, uncivil, ungracious *opposites:* courteous, polite
absence	*noun*	1 absenteeism, non-appearance, non-attendance, non-existence, truancy *opposites:* attendance, existence, presence
		2 deficiency, lack, scarcity, want *opposite:* sufficiency
absent	*adj*	away, elsewhere, far away, gone, missing, not present, truanting *opposites:* in attendance, on hand, present
absent-minded	*adj*	dreaming, faraway, forgetful, inattentive, scatter-brained, withdrawn *opposites:* alert, attentive, on the ball, switched-on
absolute	*adj*	1 complete, final, full, total, utmost, utter *opposites:* incomplete, partial
		2 definite, out-and-out, outright, perfect, pure, unlimited *opposites:* conditional, depending on
absorb	*verb*	1 consume, devour, digest, drink in, receive, retain, soak up, suck up, take in *opposites:* expel, reject, spit out
		2 assimilate, take in, take on board, understand
abstain	*verb*	avoid, forego, give up, reject, renounce, shun *opposites:* enjoy, indulge
abstract	*adj*	complex, general, indefinite, philosophical, theoretical, unpractical *opposites:* concrete, definite, particular

| | *verb* | abridge, compress, extract, outline, separate, shorten, summarise, take out, withdraw |
| | | *opposites:* draw out in detail, expand, flesh out |

absurd *adj* crazy, farcical, foolish, idiotic, illogical, irrational, ludicrous, meaningless, nonsensical, preposterous, ridiculous, unreasonable

opposites: logical, meaningful, rational, sensible

absurdity *noun* farce, folly, foolishness, irrationality, meaninglessness, nonsense, stupidity

abundance *noun* fullness, glut, good supply, heap, plenty, profusion, riches, richness, wealth

opposites: dearth, lack, scarcity

abundant *adj* copious, exuberant, full, lavish, luxuriant, overflowing, plentiful, profuse, rich, teeming, well-provided, well-supplied

opposites: limited, mean, scarce, sparse, thin

abuse *verb* curse, damage, harm, hurt, ill-treat, injure, insult, maltreat, misuse, take advantage of, violate, wrong

opposites: care for, cherish, look after, praise

noun blame, damage, ill-treatment, injury, misuse, wrong, wrongdoing

opposites: attention, care, kindness

accelerate *verb* advance, hasten, hurry, increase speed, quicken, speed up, step up

opposites: decelerate, delay, slow down

accept *verb* 1 gain, get, obtain, receive, take

opposites: give up, hand over, release

2 abide by, acknowledge, agree to, approve, believe, consent to, recognise, submit to, tolerate

opposites: refuse, reject

access	*noun*	approach, channel, door, doorway, entrance, passage, opening
	verb	obtain, recover, retrieve
accident	*noun*	1 blow, casualty, collision, disaster, injury, mishap
		2 bad luck, chance, fate, misfortune
accommodate	*verb*	1 aid, assist, cater for, help, oblige, provide for, serve, suit, supply
		2 harbour, house, lodge, provide shelter for, put up, shelter
accompany	*verb*	be a companion to, escort, go with, support
		opposites: abandon, leave
accomplice	*noun*	ally, collaborator, helper, henchman, partner in crime
accomplish	*verb*	achieve, bring about, bring off, carry out, do, finish, fulfil, manage, perform, produce, realise
account	*noun*	1 description, narrative, report, statement, story
		2 bill, cheque, invoice, statement, tab
		3 cause, explanation, motive, reason
		4 significance, value, worth
	verb	believe, judge, regard, think
account for	*verb*	1 answer for, clear up, explain, justify
		2 destroy, kill, put paid to
accumulate	*verb*	assemble, build up, collect, gather, pile up, store
accuracy	*noun*	correctness, exactness, precision, truth, truthfulness
		opposites: imprecision, inaccuracy
accurate	*adj*	correct, exact, faithful, honest, precise, regular, reliable, right, true
		opposites: inaccurate, incorrect, wrong
accuse	*verb*	blame, denounce, inform against
ache	*verb*	hurt, pain, suffer, throb, twinge
achieve	*verb*	accomplish, bring about, carry out, complete, finish, gain, obtain, realise, succeed in, win

acknowledge   *verb*   accept, admit, concede, confirm, grant, recognise, vouch for

opposites: deny, disavow, reject

acquaintance   *noun*   associate, colleague

acquainted with   *adj*   aware of, familiar with, informed, informed of

acquire   *verb*   amass, collect, gain, gather, get, obtain, procure, receive, win

act   *noun*   1 accomplishment, achievement, deed, exploit, feat

2 fake, make-believe, performance, pretence, sham, show

verb   1 behave, carry out, execute, make, operate, perform, work

2 feign, mimic, portray, pretend, seem

action   *noun*   1 act, deed, exploit, feat, operation, performance

2 activity, exercise, exertion, motion, movement, work

opposites: inaction, inactivity

3 battle, conflict, fighting, warfare

active   *adj*   agile, alert, brisk, busy, energetic, hard-working, industrious, lively, nimble, quick, sprightly, vigorous

opposites: dull, lazy, lifeless

actual   *adj*   concrete, definite, factual, genuine, real, true, unquestionable

opposites: abstract, indefinite, unreal

actually   *adv*   indeed, in fact, in reality, literally, really, truly

acute   *adj*   1 clever, keen, perceptive, sensitive, sharp, shrewd, smart, subtle

opposites: dull, obtuse, stupid

2 critical, crucial, dangerous, extreme, grave, serious

opposites: harmless, mild, non-serious, not serious

3 peaked, pointed, sharp

opposites: flat, obtuse

adamant	*adj*	determined, firm, inflexible, insistent, obdurate, stubborn, unshakeable
		opposites: easygoing, flexible, yielding
adapt	*verb*	acclimatise, adjust, alter, change, conform, fit, match, remodel, suit
add	*verb*	attach, combine, include, join, tack on
		opposites: detach, remove, subtract
addition	*noun*	adding, attachment, enlargement, extension, increase, supplement
		opposite: subtraction
address	*noun*	1 place, residence
		2 lecture, speech, sermon, talk
	verb	1 put an address on (a letter etc.)
		2 greet, hail, lecture to, speak to, talk to
adequate	*adj*	acceptable, fair, good enough, passable, presentable, satisfactory, sufficient, suitable
		opposites: inadequate, insufficient, unacceptable, unsatisfactory
adhesive	*adj*	clinging, sticking, sticky, tacky
	noun	glue, paste
adjacent	*adj*	adjoining, alongside, beside, bordering, close, near, neighbouring, next, touching
adjust	*verb*	adapt, alter, arrange, change, fit, modify, remodel, reshape
		opposites: leave alone, leave unaltered
admiration	*noun*	adoration, approval, esteem, praise, respect, wonder, worship
admire	*verb*	adore, appreciate, approve, praise, respect, value
		opposites: despise, dislike
admission	*noun*	1 access, admittance, entrance, entry
		opposites: exit, way out

                2 admitting, confession, declaration
                   opposites: denial, exclusion

admit   *verb* 1 accept, agree, concede, confess, reveal
                   opposites: deny, reject

                2 allow to enter, give access to, let in
                   opposite: show out

adopt   *verb* accept, choose, follow, select, support, take up
                 opposites: disown, repudiate

adore   *verb* admire, dote on, glorify, honour, idolise, love,
                 worship
                 opposites: hate, loathe, revile

adult   *adj* developed, full-grown, grown-up, mature
                 opposites: immature, young

advance   *verb* 1 go ahead, go forward, move on, press on, progress
                   opposites: retreat, withdraw

                2 bring forward, offer, present, provide, supply
                   opposites: put back, take back

                3 lend, pay beforehand

          noun 1 development, growth, headway, improvement,
                   progress
                2 deposit, down payment, loan

advantage   *noun* 1 benefit, blessing, gain, help, profit, usefulness
                   opposites: disadvantage, hindrance, loss

                2 edge, superiority, sway, upper hand

adventurous   *adj* bold, daring, impetuous, intrepid, plucky,
                 swashbuckling
                 opposites: careful, cautious, timid

adversary   *noun* attacker, competitor, enemy, opponent, rival
                 opposites: ally, supporter

advertise	*verb*	announce, broadcast, declare, display, inform, make known, notify, proclaim, publish
advice	*noun*	counsel, guidance, help, information, instruction, notification, opinion
advise	*verb*	forewarn, guide, inform, instruct, notify, urge, warn
affair	*noun*	1 activity, business, event, happening, incident, matter, occurrence, operation, project, topic, undertaking
		2 relationship, romance
affect	*verb*	alter, change, influence, involve, modify, transform, upset
affected	*adj*	insincere, pompous, pretentious
		opposites: genuine, natural, sincere
affection	*noun*	attachment, fondness, good will, liking, love, regard, tenderness, warmth
		opposites: dislike, hate
afford	*verb*	be able to buy, have enough money to buy, spare
afraid	*adj*	alarmed, anxious, fearful, frightened, nervous, scared, timid, uneasy
		opposites: brave, confident, fearless
age	*noun*	1 era, lifetime, long time, period, span
		opposites: instant, minute, moment, second
		2 elderliness, maturity, old age, seniority
		opposite: youth
	verb	grow old, mature, ripen
agent	*noun*	deputy, go-between, operator, representative, substitute
aggressive	*adj*	hostile, offensive, pushing, pushy, quarrelsome
		opposites: mild-mannered, peaceable, submissive, weak

agile	*adj*	active, brisk, lively, nimble, quick, sharp, sprightly, spry, supple
		opposites: clumsy, inactive, stiff
agitate	*verb*	1 beat, churn, excite, shake, stir, toss
		2 alarm, disturb, incite, stimulate, trouble, upset, worry
agony	*noun*	anguish, distress, misery, pain, suffering, torment, torture
		opposites: ecstasy, joy
agree	*verb*	1 allow, permit, see eye to eye, side (with), yield
		opposites: disagree, refuse, resist
		2 coincide, correspond, match, suit
agreeable	*adj*	attractive, delightful, enjoyable, likeable, pleasant, pleasing, satisfying
		opposites: disagreeable, distasteful, nasty
agreement	*noun*	1 arrangement, bargain, contract, pact, settlement, treaty, understanding
		2 accord, harmony, unanimity, union
		opposites: disagreement, disharmony
aid	*verb*	assist, befriend, help, relieve, serve, support
		opposites: abandon, desert, leave unaided
	noun	assistance, benefit, favour, help, relief, service, support
aim	*noun*	design, desire, end, goal, hope, intention, objective, plan, purpose, target, wish
	verb	1 point (at a target), set your sights (on), take aim, target
		2 attempt, intend, plan, resolve, seek, want, wish
air	*noun*	1 atmosphere, breeze, oxygen, sky, wind
		2 appearance, impression, look, manner, style, tone

alarm	*noun*	1	alarm-bell, alert, distress-signal, siren, warning sound
		2	anxiety, consternation, dismay, distress, fear, panic, scare, terror, unease
			opposites: calm, composure, ease of mind
	verb		frighten, scare, startle, terrify, terrorise
			opposites: calm, reassure, soothe
alert	*adj*	1	active, brisk, lively, nimble, quick, sprightly
			opposites: inactive, sleepy
		2	careful, observant, on the look out, perceptive, sharp-witted, wary, wide-awake
			opposites: dull, listless, slow
alive	*adj*	1	breathing, existing, in existence, live, living
			opposites: dead, deceased
		2	active, eager, lively, quick, spry, vigorous, vital
			opposites: dull, lifeless
allow	*verb*		accept, admit, agree, approve, authorise, concede, confess, grant, let, permit, tolerate
			opposites: deny, disallow, forbid, refuse, turn down
alter	*verb*		change, modify, remodel, reshape, vary
altogether	*adv*		all in all, as a whole, completely, generally, in general, on the whole, totally, utterly
amaze	*verb*		astonish, astound, shock, startle, surprise
amazement	*noun*		astonishment, bewilderment, surprise, wonder
ambition	*noun*		aim, desire, dream, goal, hope, intent, purpose, target
ambitious	*adj*		bold, enterprising, go-ahead, keen, purposeful, striving, zealous
			opposites: contented, unambitious

amiable	*adj*	charming, cheerful, delightful, friendly, likeable, lovable, sociable
		opposites: hostile, unfriendly
amount	*noun*	cost, mass, measure, number, quantity, sum, total, volume
amount to	*verb*	add up to, come to, equal, total
amuse	*verb*	cheer up, delight, entertain, make laugh or smile, please
		opposites: bore, depress, fail to please
ancient	*adj*	old, old-fashioned, original, out-of-date, prehistoric, primeval
		opposites: modern, up-to-date
anger	*noun*	annoyance, fury, irritation, outrage, rage, temper, wrath
angle	*noun*	1 bend, corner, point
		2 approach, perspective, point of view, slant, viewpoint
angry	*adj*	cross, displeased, fuming, hot under the collar, irate
animal	*noun*	1 beast, creature, mammal
		2 barbarian, beast, brute, monster
announce	*verb*	declare, make known, proclaim, publish, report, reveal, state
		opposites: hide, keep quiet, suppress
annoy	*verb*	anger, bother, displease, enrage, irritate, madden, pester, provoke, tease
		opposites: gratify, please
annual	*adj*	coming every year, yearly
anonymous	*adj*	impersonal, nameless, unidentified, unknown, unnamed, unspecified
		opposites: distinctive, known, named

answer	*noun*	1 reply, response
		2 defence, explanation, result, solution
	verb	acknowledge, explain, reply, respond
anticipate	*verb*	count upon, expect, hope for, look forward to, predict
anxiety	*noun*	concern, distress, dread, nervousness, torment, torture, worry
		opposites: calm, composure
anxious	*adj*	afraid, apprehensive, concerned, fearful, nervous, tense, uneasy, worried
		opposites: calm, composed, untroubled
apparent	*adj*	clear, distinct, noticeable, obvious, open, plain, visible
		opposites: concealed, hidden, real
appeal to	*verb*	1 ask, plead, request
		2 attract, fascinate, interest, please
		opposites: displease, fail to attract
appear	*verb*	1 become visible, come into sight, come into view, emerge, show up, surface
		opposites: disappear, go out of sight
		2 look, seem
appearance	*noun*	character, expression, figure, look, manner
applaud	*verb*	approve, cheer, clap, congratulate, encourage, praise
		opposites: boo, criticise
apply	*verb*	cover with, lay on, place, put on, rub, smear, spread on
		opposites: remove, rub off, take off
apply for	*verb*	ask for, claim, make an application for, request
apply yourself	*verb*	buckle down, commit yourself, concentrate, persevere, study

appreciation	*noun*	1 admiration, enjoyment, liking, praise, respect, thanks

opposites: blame, disrespect, ingratitude

2 awareness, knowledge, recognition, understanding

opposites: ignorance, lack of understanding

3 growth in value, increase in value

opposites: depreciation, fall in value

approach   *verb*   1 advance towards, come close, come near, draw near, gain on, meet

opposites: draw back, go away from, retreat from

2 apply to, make advances to, mention, sound out

noun   1 access, entrance, way in

2 advance, offer, proposal

appropriate   *adj*   apt, correct, fit, fitting, proper, relevant, suitable, well-chosen

opposites: ill-chosen, incorrect, unsuitable

approve   *verb*   agree to, allow, authorise, consent to, like, permit, recommend, support, uphold

opposites: disapprove, reject

apt   *adj*   appropriate, correct, fit, fitting, proper, relevant, suitable, timely

opposites: incorrect, unsuitable

argue   *verb*   debate, differ, discuss, dispute

opposite: agree

argument   *noun*   1 disagreement, dispute, quarrel, squabble

opposite: agreement

2 case, claim, plea, subject, theme

aroma   *noun*   bouquet, fragrance, odour, perfume, scent, smell

arouse	*verb*	awaken, excite, inflame, provoke, rouse, stir up, wake up
		opposites: calm down, quieten, relax
arrange	*verb*	1 classify, group, put in order, set out, sort out
		opposites: disturb, upset
		2 cause to happen, devise, organise, plan, prepare
arrangement	*noun*	1 agreement, deal, settlement, terms
		2 grouping, layout, method, ordering, organisation, plan, structure
arrest	*verb*	apprehend, capture, catch, grasp, seize, take prisoner
		opposites: let go, release
art	*noun*	1 artistry, craft, expertise, knack, knowledge, skill
		2 drawing, painting, sculpture
article	*noun*	1 element, item, object, piece, thing, unit
		2 essay, feature, piece, written account
artificial	*adj*	man-made, manufactured, synthetic, unnatural
		opposites: genuine, natural, real
artistic	*adj*	creative, elegant, imaginative, sensitive, stylish, tasteful
		opposites: clumsy, coarse, inelegant, unimaginative
ascend	*verb*	climb, go up, mount, move up, rise, soar, take off
		opposites: descend, go down
ashamed	*adj*	blushing, embarrassed, humiliated, shame-faced, sorry
		opposites: defiant, proud
ask	*verb*	inquire, interrogate, question, quiz
ask for	*verb*	demand, implore, order, request, require, summon
assault	*verb*	attack, hit, set upon, strike

assemble	*verb*	1 build, construct, erect, set up
		opposites: disassemble, take apart, take down
		2 collect, gather, round up, summon together
		opposites: dismiss, disperse, scatter
assist	*verb*	aid, help, serve, support
		opposites: hamper, hinder
assistance	*noun*	aid, backing, benefit, boost, cooperation, help, relief, support
		opposites: hindrance, holding-back, non-cooperation
assistant	*noun*	accomplice, ally, colleague, helper
assortment	*noun*	collection, grouping, jumble, mixture, selection, variety
assume	*verb*	believe, expect, imagine, presume, suppose, take for granted, understand
		opposite: know for sure
assure	*verb*	convince, ensure, guarantee, persuade, promise
astonish	*verb*	amaze, astound, baffle, shock, startle, stun, surprise
astounding	*adj*	amazing, astonishing, breathtaking, striking, stunning, surprising
		opposites: ordinary, unremarkable
astray	*adv*	adrift, awry, lost, off course, off the rails, wrong
attach	*verb*	1 adhere, affix, bind, combine, connect, fasten, fix, join, secure, stick
		opposites: detach, unfasten
		2 add, append, tack on
		opposites: remove, take away

attack	*noun*	1 assault, bombardment, invasion, offensive, onslaught, raid
		2 fit, seizure, spasm
	verb	assault, blame, criticise, denounce, invade, lash out, set about, set on, strike, wade into
attempt	*verb*	tackle, try, undertake
	noun	bid, endeavour, try, undertaking
attention	*noun*	awareness, care, heed, notice, respect, thought
		opposites: disregard, inattention
attract	*verb*	interest, please, tempt
		opposites: repel, turn off
attraction	*noun*	1 allure, appeal, charm, fascination, interest
		2 draw, inducement, invitation, lure, magnetism, temptation
		3 entertainment, event, show
attractive	*adj*	appealing, beautiful, charming, fascinating, gorgeous, handsome, lovely, pleasing, pretty
		opposites: plain, ugly, unattractive
audacity	*noun*	boldness, cheek, courage, foolhardiness, impertinence, nerve
		opposites: caution, cowardice, timidity
audience	*noun*	assembly, congregation, crowd, following, gathering, meeting, public, spectators
authentic	*adj*	accurate, actual, factual, genuine, pure, real, true, valid
		opposites: counterfeit, fake, impure
author	*noun*	creator, designer, founder, maker, originator, planner, writer
authority	*noun*	1 administration, government, management, power, supremacy
		2 licence, permission, permit, right

available	*adj*	accessible, at hand, convenient, on tap, within reach
average	*noun*	mean, medium, midpoint, norm, par, standard
		opposites: exception, extreme
	adj	common, everyday, mediocre, ordinary, unremarkable, usual
		opposites: abnormal, exceptional, extraordinary, unusual
avoid	*verb*	bypass, dodge, escape, keep away from, shun, steer clear of
		opposites: approach, look out for
awake	*adj*	alert, alive, aware, observant, vigilant, watchful
		opposites: asleep, careless, unaware
award	*noun*	decoration, gift, grant, prize, trophy
aware	*adj*	conscious, knowing, knowledgeable, sharp, shrewd
		opposites: insensitive, unaware
awful	*adj*	dreadful, hideous, horrible, horrific, shocking, terrible, unpleasant
		opposites: good, pleasant
awkward	*adj*	clumsy, difficult, ungainly, unhelpful, unpleasant
		opposites: convenient, elegant, graceful, neat

B

babble	*verb*	chatter, mumble, murmur, mutter
babyish	*adj*	childish, infantile, immature, silly
back	*noun*	end, rear, reverse
		opposite: front
	verb	1 assist, encourage, side with, support
		opposites: discourage, oppose
		2 go backwards, reverse
backward	*adj*	dull, hesitant, shy, slow, underdeveloped
		opposites: bold, forward, precocious
backwards	*adv*	in reverse, rearward
		opposite: forwards
bad	*adj*	1 badly-behaved, evil, harmful, immoral, naughty, unpleasant, wicked, wrong
		opposites: good, moral
		2 defective, faulty, imperfect, incorrect, inferior, spoilt, unpleasant, unsatisfactory
		opposites: good, in good condition, satisfactory
		3 ill, painful, sick, upset
		opposites: in good health, well
badge	*noun*	emblem, identification, insignia, sign, trademark
bad-tempered	*adj*	cross, irascible, irritable
		opposites: genial, good-humoured
baffle	*verb*	astound, bewilder, confuse, mystify, puzzle
		opposites: enlighten, inform, instruct
balance	*verb*	1 equalise, equate, make equal
		2 assess, compare, consider, estimate, weigh, weigh up

	noun	composure, equilibrium, stability, steadiness
		opposites: imbalance, instability
ball	*noun*	1 globe, orb, sphere
		2 dance, social gathering
ban	*verb*	banish, bar, blacklist, exclude, forbid, prohibit, suppress
		opposites: include, permit
	noun	boycott, condemnation, embargo, prohibition
bandit	*noun*	desperado, gangster, highwayman, hijacker, outlaw, pirate, robber, thief
band together	*verb*	ally, collaborate, gather together, group, join together, merge, unite
		opposites: disband, disperse, fall out, split up
bang	*noun*	1 blow, bump, clash, collision, crash, knock, punch, smack, thump, whack
		2 clang, clap, noise, peal, report, slam, thud
	verb	1 bump, crash, explode, hammer, knock, pound, slam, stamp, strike, thump
		2 clang, clatter, peal, resound, thunder
banish	*verb*	ban, bar, deport, eject, evict, exclude, expel, get rid of, remove, shut out
		opposites: bring back, recall, welcome back
bar	*noun*	1 barricade, barrier, hindrance, obstacle, obstruction
		2 pole, rod, shaft, stick
		3 inn, pub, public house, saloon, tavern

bare	*adj*	1 bald, naked, nude, stripped, unclothed, undressed
		opposites: clothed, covered, dressed, hairy
		2 barren, empty, essential, poor, simple, spare, stark, vacant
		opposites: complicated, elaborate
barely	*adv*	almost, hardly, just, scarcely, sparingly
bargain	*noun*	1 negotiation, pact, promise, understanding
		2 good deal, snip
barren	*adj*	arid, dry, dull, empty, infertile, unproductive
		opposites: fertile, productive, rich
barrier	*noun*	barricade, hindrance, hurdle, obstruction, restriction, wall
base	*noun*	bottom, core, foundation, origin, starting-point, support
	verb	build, construct, establish, locate, place, station
basis	*noun*	1 base, bottom, core, foundation
		2 main ingredient, main part
battle	*noun*	attack, campaign, clash, conflict, contest, dispute, fight, strife, struggle, war
beam	*noun*	1 bar, girder, plank, rafter, shaft, support
		2 gleam, glimmer, glint, ray, shaft
	verb	1 glimmer, glitter, glow, shine
		2 grin, laugh, smile
		3 broadcast, emit, transmit
bear	*verb*	1 carry, convey, maintain, shoulder, support, transport, undergo, uphold
		2 abide, endure, permit, put up with, suffer, tolerate

beast	*noun*	1 animal, brute, creature
		2 devil, fiend, monster, savage, swine
beat	*verb*	1 bang, batter, hit, lash, pound, punch, slap, thrash, whip
		2 conquer, defeat, overcome, overwhelm, subdue, vanquish
		3 flutter, pound, quake, quiver, shake, throb, thump, tremble, vibrate
beautiful	*adj*	appealing, attractive, delightful, good-looking, gorgeous, lovely, stunning
		opposites: plain, ugly, unattractive
before	*adv*	ahead, earlier, formerly, in advance, in front, previously, sooner
befriend	*verb*	aid, assist, favour, help, stand by, support, uphold
		opposites: alienate, neglect, oppose
beg	*verb*	beseech, crave, implore, plead, pray, request, scrounge
begin	*verb*	commence, initiate, introduce, originate, start
		opposites: conclude, end, finish
behave	*verb*	act, operate, perform, respond, work
behind	*adv*	after, afterwards, following, next, subsequently
belief	*noun*	conviction, creed, doctrine, faith, notion, opinion, principle, theory
		opposites: disbelief, doubt, uncertainty
belong	*verb*	be connected with, be part of, go with, tie up with
belongings	*noun*	gear, goods, possessions, stuff, things
below	*adv*	beneath, lower, lower down, under, underneath

bend	*verb*	curve, mould, shape, turn, twist, veer
	noun	angle, bow, corner, curve, loop, turn, twist
beneath	*adv*	below, inferior to, lower than, subject to, under
benefit	*noun*	advantage, aid, blessing, boon, favour, help, profit, service
		opposites: disadvantage, harm, hindrance
benevolent	*adj*	charitable, generous, helpful, kind-hearted, magnanimous
		opposites: ill-disposed, miserly, unhelpful
besides	*adv*	also, as well, extra, furthermore, in addition, moreover
best	*adj*	finest, first, first rate, greatest, highest, largest, perfect, supreme
bet	*noun*	gamble, stake, venture, wager
	verb	bid, chance, gamble, risk, speculate, venture, wager
better	*adj*	finer, fitter, healthier, improving, preferable, progressing, superior
		opposites: poorer, worse
	verb	beat, exceed, go further than, improve on, outdo, out-strip, surpass
betterment	*noun*	advancement, improvement, welfare
bewilder	*verb*	baffle, bamboozle, confuse, daze, muddle, mystify, puzzle
biased	*adj*	bigoted, one-sided, prejudiced, unfair
		opposites: fair, impartial, unbiased
bicker	*verb*	argue, disagree, dispute, quarrel, row, squabble
		opposite: agree
bid	*noun*	attempt, effort, offer, proposal, proposition, try

big   *adj*   bulky, colossal, gigantic, great, huge, immense, large, massive, substantial, vast

opposites: little, small, tiny

big-headed   *adj*   boastful, conceited, proud, vain

opposites: humble, meek, modest

bill   *noun*   1 account, invoice, reckoning, statement, tab, tally

2 circular, hand-bill, hand-out, leaflet, notice, poster, programme, sheet

bind   *verb*   fasten, hold together, join, marry, tie together, unite

opposites: set free, unbind, unfasten, untie

bit   *noun*   chip, crumb, fragment, iota, morsel, part, piece, scrap, segment, slice

bite   *verb*   1 chew, crunch, gnaw, nibble

2 pierce, rend, seize, snap

bitter   *adj*   1 acid, acrid, biting, sharp, sour, unsweetened, vinegary

opposites: pleasant-tasting, sweet

2 cruel, embittered, harsh, hateful, hostile, merciless, ruthless, sarcastic, severe

opposites: contented, good-natured, pleasant

black   *adj*   dark, ebony, jet, pitch black

blame   *noun*   censure, condemnation, criticism, fault, guilt

     verb   accuse, condemn, criticise, find fault with, reprimand

opposites: applaud, commend, praise

blank   *adj*   clear, expressionless, impassive, plain, vacant

opposites: expressive, lively

blaze	*noun*	brilliance, fire, flame, flames, flare-up
	verb	burn, erupt, explode, flame, flare-up, flash, shine
bleak	*adj*	bare, barren, cheerless, depressing, desolate, dismal, dreary, empty, gloomy, grim
		opposites: attractive, bright, cheerful, interesting, promising
blind	*adj*	1 sightless, unseeing, unsighted
		opposites: seeing, sighted
		2 careless, heedless, ignorant, insensitive, thoughtless
		opposites: aware, clear-sighted
block	*noun*	1 bar, brick, cake, chunk, cube, lump, piece, square
		2 barrier, blockage, hindrance, obstacle, stoppage
	verb	hinder, obstruct, oppose, prevent, stop
blood-thirsty	*adj*	barbaric, brutal, cruel, ferocious, fierce, savage
		opposites: civilised, gentle, peaceful
blossom	*noun*	bloom, flower, flowers
	verb	bloom, develop, flourish, flower, grow, mature, prosper, thrive
		opposites: die, fade away, wilt, wither
blot	*noun*	blotch, fault, flaw, mark, smear, spot, stain
blow	*noun*	1 clout, knock, punch, smack, whack
		2 bombshell, disappointment, disaster, misfortune, reverse, setback, shock
blue	*adj*	azure, indigo, navy blue, royal blue, sapphire, turquoise
blunder	*noun*	error, fault, mistake, slip
	verb	bungle, err, misjudge, stumble

blurred	*adj*	dim, faint, fuzzy, hazy, indistinct, misty, vague
		opposites: clear, distinct, well-defined
boast	*verb*	brag, crow, exaggerate, show off, talk big
		opposites: play down, speak modestly
body	*noun*	1 being, corpse, creature, human, individual
		2 association, company, organisation, system
boil	*verb*	1 brew, bubble, froth, seethe, steam
		2 erupt, explode, fume, rage
bold	*adj*	adventurous, brave, daring, fearless, heroic, lively, reckless
		opposites: afraid, nervous, shy, timid
bond	*noun*	agreement, binding agreement, contract, pledge, promise, word
bonus	*noun*	benefit, dividend, extra, gift, reward
		opposites: deduction, disadvantage
border	*noun*	boundary, edge, limit, margin, perimeter
bore	*noun*	annoyance, nuisance, pain in the neck, pest
		opposites: interesting person, pleasure
	verb	1 be a nuisance, be uninteresting
		opposites: amuse, interest
		2 burrow, drill, penetrate, pierce
bother	*verb*	annoy, disturb, pester, trouble, upset
		opposites: please, put at ease
	noun	annoyance, difficulty, nuisance, trouble
boundless	*adj*	countless, endless, immense, infinite, vast
		opposites: limited, finite
box	*noun*	carton, casket, chest, coffin, container, trunk

boycott	*verb*	avoid, disregard, ignore, shun
		opposites: encourage, make friends with, support
branch	*noun*	1 department, office, section, subdivision
		2 arm, limb, offshoot, shoot
brave	*adj*	bold, courageous, fearless, heroic, unafraid
		opposites: cowardly, timid
brawl	*verb*	fight, quarrel, squabble
break	*verb*	crack, damage, fracture, shatter
break down	*verb*	collapse, crush, demolish, fail, seize up
brief	*adj*	concise, pithy, short, succinct
		opposites: long, long-winded
bright	*adj*	1 blazing, brilliant, dazzling, glittering, radiant, shining
		opposites: dim, dull, faded
		2 astute, clever, intelligent, observant, quick-witted
		opposites: backward, dull, slow, stupid
		3 cheerful, happy, lively, vivacious
		opposites: apathetic, depressed, listless
brilliant	*adj*	1 blazing, dazzling, glittering, sparkling, star-like
		opposites: dull, drab
		2 clever, exceptional, intelligent, skilful, talented
		opposites: dull, slow, stupid
bring	*verb*	carry, conduct, escort, fetch, lead, take, transport
bring about	*verb*	achieve, cause to happen, effect, produce
bring to mind	*verb*	recall, recollect, remember
brisk	*adj*	active, bustling, lively, quick, refreshing, sprightly
		opposites: slow, sluggish

brittle   *adj*   breakable, delicate, easily broken, fragile, frail, weak
                              opposites: durable, strong, tough

broad   *adj*   1 extensive, far-reaching, large, vast, wide, widespread
                                 opposites: confined, narrow, slim

                         2 all-embracing, comprehensive, general, universal
                                 opposites: specialised, specific, unique

broadcast   *verb*   announce, circulate, proclaim, publicise, report, transmit

brown   *adj*   auburn, brunette, mahogany, sunburnt, tanned

brutal   *adj*   brutish, cruel, inhuman, merciless, pitiless, ruthless, vicious
                                 opposites: considerate, humane, kind

build   *verb*   assemble, construct, develop, erect, make, manufacture, put up
                                 opposites: demolish, destroy, dismantle, knock down

bully   *verb*   browbeat, coerce, domineer, persecute, terrorise

bump   *verb*   bang, bounce, crash, hit, knock, strike

                 noun   bang, blow, crash, knock, rap, thud, thump

bunch   *noun*   bundle, clump, cluster, collection, quantity

burden   *noun*   1 load, weight

                         2 anxiety, responsibility, strain, stress, worry

burn   *verb*   blaze, flame, flare, ignite, incinerate, scorch, singe, toast

burst   *verb*   break, crack, explode, puncture, rupture, shatter, split, tear

                 noun   blast, discharge, explosion, gush, outburst, spurt, torrent

                 adj   broken, punctured, ruptured, split, torn

business	*noun*	1 affair, enterprise, function, matter, problem
		2 career, commerce, employment, firm, occupation, organisation, profession, trade, work
busy	*adj*	active, energetic, hard-working, industrious, lively, occupied
		opposites: idle, inactive, unemployed
buy	*verb*	acquire, purchase
		opposite: sell
bystander	*noun*	eyewitness, onlooker, passer-by, spectator, watcher, witness

cackle	*verb*	chuckle, giggle, laugh, snigger
café	*noun*	coffee-bar, restaurant, snack bar, tea-room
cage	*noun*	aviary, coop, enclosure, pen, prison
	verb	confine, fence in, imprison, lock up, shut up
		opposites: free, release, set free
calculate	*verb*	compute, consider, count, estimate, plan, reckon, value, work out
call	*verb*	1 announce, cry, declare, greet, proclaim, shout, yell
		2 assemble, gather, invite, summon
		3 phone, telephone
	noun	1 cry, scream, shout, signal, yell
		2 announcement, command, invitation, notice, request
calm	*adj*	composed, cool, laid-back, peaceful, placid, quiet, relaxed, serene, still, unruffled, untroubled
		opposites: agitated, nervous, on edge
cancel	*verb*	cross out, delete, eliminate, erase, obliterate, strike out
		opposites: approve, keep, restore
capable	*adj*	clever, competent, efficient, gifted, intelligent, skilful, talented
		opposites: ham-fisted, incompetent, useless
capsize	*verb*	keel over, overturn, turn over, upset
captive	*noun*	convict, detainee, hostage, prisoner, slave
capture	*verb*	arrest, catch, imprison, seize, take, trap
		opposites: free, let go, release, set free
	noun	arrest, imprisonment, seizure
car	*noun*	automobile, motor-car, vehicle
care	*noun*	1 attention, caution, consideration, trouble, wariness
		opposites: inattention, carelessness, thoughtlessness
		2 anxiety, concern, stress, trouble, worry

career	*noun*	calling, employment, job, livelihood, occupation, work
careful	*adj*	accurate, cautious, painstaking, prudent, thoughtful, wary
careless	*adj*	heedless, lackadaisical, negligent, slipshod, uncaring, unthinking
cargo	*noun*	baggage, contents, freight, load, shipment
carry	*verb*	convey, fetch, move, transport
case	*noun*	1 box, container, holder, trunk
		2 event, example, instance, position
		3 action, dispute, lawsuit, trial
cash	*noun*	banknotes, change, coins, currency, funds, money
cast	*verb*	1 fling, hurl, scatter, throw, toss
		2 drop, drop off, let fall, shed
		3 form, mould, shape
	noun	actors, characters, company, performers, players
casual	*adj*	1 easygoing, informal, relaxed, unconcerned
		opposites: formal, painstaking
		2 chance, informal, spontaneous, unforeseen
		opposites: deliberate, planned
casualty	*noun*	death, injury, loss, victim, wounded
catch	*verb*	1 grab, grip, hold, seize, take
		2 arrest, capture, ensnare, entrap
		opposites: free, let go, release
cause	*verb*	bring about, effect, give rise to, induce, make happen, produce, result in
	noun	origin, purpose, reason
cautious	*adj*	careful, guarded, prudent, wary
		opposites: careless, heedless, imprudent

cease	*verb*	conclude, discontinue, end, finish, stop
		opposites: begin, initiate, start
celebrate	*verb*	1 make merry, rejoice
		2 glorify, honour, praise
central	*adj*	1 inner, median, middle, midway
		opposites: outer, peripheral ·
		2 chief, essential, focal, main, principal, vital
		opposites: marginal, minor
centre	*noun*	core, heart, kernel, middle, mid-point
		opposites: edge, outskirts
ceremony	*noun*	celebration, event, function, parade, ritual, show
certain	*adj*	1 assured, definite, fixed, precise, sure, unmistakeable
		opposites: doubtful, dubious, uncertain, unsure
		2 individual, particular, specific
certificate	*noun*	award, diploma, document, licence, qualification
challenge	*noun*	dare, obstacle, question, test, trial
	verb	confront, dare, defy, provoke, question, test
champion	*noun*	1 conqueror, hero, victor, winner
		opposites: also-ran, loser
		2 backer, defender, protector, upholder
chance	*noun*	1 gamble, risk, uncertainty
		opposites: certainty, sure thing
		2 fate, fortune, luck, providence
change	*verb*	alter, modify, reorganise, replace, substitute, swap, vary
		opposites: stay the same, maintain
	noun	1 alteration, shift, substitution, variation
		2 coins, loose money

chaos   *noun*   anarchy, confusion, disorder, muddle, pandemonium, turmoil
opposites: order, system

character   *noun*   1 disposition, make-up, nature, personality, type

            2 honour, integrity, reputation

            3 person (in a story, play or film)

charge   *noun*   1 assault, attack, rush, stampede

            2 accusation, allegation

            3 amount, cost, expenditure, price, rate

       verb   1 attack, rush, storm

            2 accuse, blame

charm   *verb*   1 attract, delight, please
opposites: displease, repel

            2 bewitch, enchant, mesmerise

       noun   1 allure, appeal, attraction, fascination, magnetism
opposites: dullness, lack of sparkle

            2 amulet, spell, talisman

chart   *noun*   diagram, graph, map, plan

       verb   draw up, map out, outline, sketch

chat   *noun*   gossip, talk, tête-à-tête

       verb   converse with, gossip, talk

cheap   *adj*   1 economical, inexpensive, low-cost, low-priced
opposites: costly, dear, expensive

            2 inferior, paltry, poor, second-rate, shoddy, vulgar
opposites: excellent, high-class, superior

cheat   *verb*   deceive, defraud, double-cross, swindle

       noun   deceiver, fraudster, imposter, swindler

check   *verb*   1 compare, examine, inspect, investigate, test, verify

            2 halt, hinder, impede, obstruct, restrain, stop

       noun   1 examination, inspection, scrutiny, test

		2 curb, disappointment, impediment, obstruction, stoppage
cheek	*noun*	audacity, impertinence, impudence, insolence, lip
cheeky	*adj*	disrespectful, impertinent, impudent, insolent
		opposites: polite, respectful
cheer	*verb*	applaud, hail, shout for
		opposites: boo, jeer
cheer up	*verb*	comfort, console, encourage, uplift, warm
		opposites: depress, discourage, dishearten
chew	*verb*	bite on, gnaw, munch
chief	*adj*	central, largest, leading, main, primary, principal, supreme
		opposites: minor, lesser, secondary, unimportant
	noun	captain, chieftain, commander, leader, master, principal
child	*noun*	baby, boy, girl, infant, offspring
chill	*verb*	cool, freeze, refrigerate
		opposites: heat, warm
	noun	cold, coldness
		opposites: heat, warmth
	adj	bleak, chilly, cold, freezing, wintry
		opposites: hot, warm
chip	*verb*	chisel, damage, nick, scratch
	noun	flake, fragment, scrap, shaving, sliver
choke	*verb*	1 block, close off, constrict, obstruct, stop
		opposites: clear, give access to, open up
		2 stifle, suffocate, throttle
choose	*verb*	pick out, select, single out, vote for
		opposites: disregard, reject, throw out

chop	*verb*	cut, hack, hew, slice
chop up	*verb*	cut up, dice, slice up
chore	*noun*	boring job, menial job, task
circle	*verb*	curve round, encompass, envelop, ring, surround
	noun	band, coil, revolution, ring
civil	*adj*	courteous, polite, refined, well-bred, well-mannered
		opposites: discourteous, ill-mannered, rude, surly
claim	*verb*	1 ask for, demand, request
		2 allege, assert, hold, state, uphold
clamp	*verb*	fasten, grip, press
		opposites: release, undo
clash	*noun*	1 collision, conflict, disagreement, fight, quarrel, showdown
		opposites: agreement, cooperation
		2 bang, clatter, noise, rattle
	verb	conflict, disagree, fight, quarrel
		opposites: agree, cooperate
clasp	*verb*	catch hold of, clutch, embrace, grasp, grip, hold, hug, seize, squeeze
	noun	brooch, buckle, fastener, hook, pin
class	*noun*	1 category, classification, family, grade, group, kind, type
		2 course, lecture, tutorial
	verb	classify, grade, group, rank, rate
clean	*adj*	1 hygienic, pure, spotless, unstained, washed
		opposites: dirty, impure, unclean, unwashed
		2 decent, good, honest, upright, virtuous
	verb	disinfect, dust, polish, purify, rinse, scrub, sponge, sweep, vacuum, wash, wipe
		opposites: dirty, mess up

clear	*adj*	1 luminous, see-through, translucent, transparent, unclouded *opposites:* cloudy, fuzzy
		2 apparent, comprehensible, evident, obvious, unmistakeable, unquestionable, well-defined *opposites:* doubtful, obscure, questionable, vague
		3 open, unimpeded, without hindrance *opposites:* blocked, restricted
	verb	1 clarify, clean, disentangle, purify, unblock, wipe *opposites:* block, muddy, obscure
		2 acquit, justify, liberate *opposites:* condemn, find guilty
clever	*adj*	bright, cunning, intelligent, quick-witted, shrewd, smart *opposites:* foolish, naive, stupid
climb	*verb*	ascend, go up, mount, rise, scale *opposites:* descend, go down
cling to	*verb*	adhere to, clasp, embrace, grasp, grip, hold, stick to
close (rhymes with 'doze')	*verb*	1 cover, lock, obstruct, shut *opposites:* open, uncover
		2 complete, conclude, end, finish, terminate *opposites:* begin, continue
close (rhymes with 'dose')	*adj*	1 nearby, neighbouring *opposites:* distant, far away
		2 humid, muggy, stifling, stuffy, suffocating
		3 dear, faithful, intimate
cloth	*noun*	1 duster, rag, towel
		2 fabric, material, textile
clothe	*verb*	cover, dress, equip, outfit *opposites:* uncover, undress

club	*noun*	1 bat, cudgel, stick, truncheon
		2 association, company, group, society
	verb	batter, beat, cudgel, hammer, hit, strike
clue	*noun*	evidence, hint, idea, inkling, notion, sign, suggestion
clumsy	*adj*	awkward, rough, ungainly
		opposites: agile, graceful, skilful
clutch	*verb*	catch, clasp, embrace, grab, grasp, seize
		opposites: let go, release, set free
coach	*noun*	1 bus, carriage
		2 instructor, teacher, trainer, tutor
	verb	drill, instruct, prepare, teach, train, tutor
coarse	*adj*	1 impure, rough, unfinished
		opposites: delicate, fine, well-finished
		2 crude, offensive, rude, vulgar
		opposites: polite, refined, well-mannered
coat	*noun*	cloak, covering, jacket, raincoat
	verb	apply, cover, plaster, smear, spread
coax	*verb*	entice, flatter, persuade, wheedle
		opposites: discourage, dissuade
coil	*noun*	curl, loop, spiral, twist, wreathe
	verb	curl, entwine, loop, twist, wind, wreathe
		opposites: straighten, untwist, unwind
cold	*adj*	1 bleak, chilly, cool, freezing, icy, wintry
		opposites: hot, warm
		2 aloof, distant, reserved, unfriendly, unsympathetic
		opposites: friendly, sympathetic
collapse	*noun*	breakdown, downfall, failure, faint, flop
	verb	break down, crumple, fail, founder, sink
collect	*verb*	acquire, amass, assemble, gather, stockpile

collide	*verb*	crash, hit, meet head on, smash into
colossal	*adj*	enormous, gigantic, huge, immense, massive, vast
		opposites: minuscule, small, tiny
colour	*noun*	hue, paint, pigment, shade, tinge, tint
	verb	dye, paint, stain, tint
combat	*noun*	battle, conflict, contest, fight, struggle, war, warfare
		opposites: peace, truce
combine	*verb*	blend, connect, join, link, merge, mix, unify
		opposites: break up, divide, separate
come	*verb*	1 approach, arrive, draw near, enter, reach
		opposites: depart, go, leave
		2 become, happen, materialise, occur
comfort	*verb*	cheer up, console, encourage, hearten, reassure
		opposites: discourage, dishearten, torment
comic	*adj*	amusing, comical, funny, humorous, jocular, witty
		opposites: serious, solemn, tragic
command	*verb*	demand, lead, manage, order, rule, supervise
	noun	decree, instruction, order, rule
commence	*verb*	begin, initiate, start
		opposites: conclude, end, finish
common	*adj*	1 commonplace, everyday, ordinary, plain, routine, standard, usual
		opposites: exceptional, noteworthy, rare, unusual
		2 cheap, coarse, inferior, low, vulgar
		opposites: genteel, refined, well-mannered
companion	*noun*	accomplice, ally, colleague, comrade, friend, partner
company	*noun*	1 assembly, community, crowd, gathering, group
		2 business, firm, partnership
		3 companions, friends, visitors

compel	*verb*	force, make, oblige, pressurise
		opposites: prevent, stop
compete	*verb*	contest, fight, oppose, struggle, vie
		opposites: assist, cooperate, help
competent	*adj*	able, capable, clever, efficient
		opposites: incompetent, inefficient, useless
complain	*verb*	groan, grumble, moan, whine, whinge
complete	*verb*	achieve, conclude, end, finish, terminate, wind up
		opposites: begin, continue, start
	adj	entire, finished, full, perfect, total, whole
		opposites: incomplete, unfinished
compliment	*noun*	congratulation, flattery, praise
		opposites: criticism, insult
	verb	admire, congratulate, flatter, praise
		opposites: condemn, insult
compose	*verb*	construct, create, devise, form, make, produce, write
conceal	*verb*	cover, disguise, hide, keep secret
		opposites: lay bare, reveal, show
conceit	*noun*	arrogance, pride, vanity
		opposites: humility, modesty
concentrate	*verb*	1 pay attention, think carefully
		opposites: be distracted, day-dream
		2 collect, draw together, gather, huddle together
		opposites: dilute, disperse, separate
conclude	*verb*	1 close, complete, end, finish, terminate
		opposites: begin, start
		2 deduce, infer, judge, reason, suppose
condemn	*verb*	blame, convict, denounce, sentence
		opposites: acquit, approve, pardon

condense   *verb*   abbreviate, compress, curtail, reduce, shorten, thicken

opposites: dilute, expand

condition   *noun*   1 case, circumstances, state, terms

2 disease, disorder, illness, state of health

3 demand, proviso, requirement, rule

conduct   *verb*   1 do, manage, organise, run, supervise, transact

2 carry, convey, direct, lead, steer, take

conduct   *noun*   actions, bearing, behaviour, demeanour, ways

confess   *verb*   admit, confirm, disclose, own up

opposite: deny

confident   *adj*   assured, self-assured, sure, unafraid

opposites: shy, timid, timorous

confidential   *adj*   private, secret

opposites: common knowledge, public

confine   *verb*   enclose, imprison, keep prisoner, shut up

opposites: release, set free

confuse   *verb*   1 jumble up, mingle, mix up, muddle, upset,

opposites: put in order, straighten out

2 bamboozle, bewilder, muddle, mystify, puzzle

opposites: enlighten, inform

confusion   *noun*   chaos, clutter, disorder, jumble, mess, mix-up, muddle, shambles, turmoil

opposite: order

connect   *verb*   attach, combine, couple, fasten, join, link, unite

opposites: separate, unfasten

conquer   *verb*   crush, defeat, master, overcome, vanquish

opposites: surrender, yield

43

consider	*verb*	believe, contemplate, examine, judge, ponder, reflect, study, think about
		opposites: dismiss, ignore
considerable	*adj*	abundant, great, important, large, significant, substantial
		opposites: insignificant, slight
considerate	*adj*	attentive, concerned, kind, thoughtful, unselfish
		opposites: selfish, thoughtless
construct	*verb*	build, create, fashion, manufacture
		opposites: demolish, destroy
consume	*verb*	1 devour, drink, eat, guzzle, swallow
		opposite: spit out
		2 drain away, expend, spend, use up, waste
		opposites: collect, gather, preserve, store up
contain	*verb*	1 comprise, enclose, hold, include
		2 check, control, limit, restrain
content	*noun*	essence, ideas, meaning, subject matter, substance, thoughts
content	*adj*	comfortable, glad, happy, pleased, relaxed, satisfied
		opposites: discontented, dissatisfied, unhappy
contest	*noun*	battle, conflict, fight, game, match, struggle
contest	*verb*	challenge, debate, dispute, fight, oppose, question
continue	*verb*	carry on, last, maintain, persevere, persist, prolong, stay
		opposites: discontinue, stop
contract	*verb*	lessen, narrow, reduce, shrink, tighten, wither
		opposites: expand, extend, lengthen
contradict	*verb*	challenge, deny, dispute, oppose
		opposites: accept, agree with, confirm

control	*verb*	1 command, direct, dominate, guide, manage, rule
		2 curb, keep a check on, limit, restrain, subdue
convenient	*adj*	handy, helpful, suitable, useful
		opposites: awkward, inconvenient, unsuitable
conversation	*noun*	chat, dialogue, discussion, talk
cool	*adj*	1 chilly, cold, unheated
		opposite: warm
		2 calm, level-headed, relaxed, unruffled
		opposites: excitable, hot-headed
		3 cold, offhand, unfriendly, unhelpful, unwelcoming
		opposites: friendly, warm
copy	*verb*	duplicate, imitate, photocopy, repeat, reproduce
core	*noun*	centre, essence, heart, kernel, nub
		opposites: exterior, outside, surface
correct	*adj*	accurate, exact, proper, right
		opposites: incorrect, wrong
correspond	*verb*	communicate, speak, write
cost	*noun*	1 amount, charge, expense, payment, price, worth
		2 damage, harm, hurt, injury, sacrifice
council	*noun*	assembly, committee, conference, parliament
count	*verb*	1 add, calculate, estimate, reckon
		2 matter, mean something, signify
courage	*noun*	boldness, bravery, heroism, spirit, valour
		opposites: cowardice, weakness
course	*noun*	1 channel, direction, path, route, track, way
		2 curriculum, programme, studies
courtesy	*noun*	consideration, manners, politeness
		opposites: discourtesy, rudeness

cover	*verb*	cloak, conceal, enclose, hide, protect, screen, shelter
		opposites: disclose, reveal, uncover
crack	*verb*	break, explode, fracture, snap, splinter
	noun	chink, cranny, crevice, fissure, gap
crafty	*adj*	cunning, deceitful, shrewd, sly
		opposites: frank, honest, sincere
cram	*verb*	compress, overfill, press, shove, stuff
crash	*noun*	accident, bang, bump, clash, collision, jolt, pile-up, smash, smash-up, thud
	verb	bang, bump, collide, smash, topple
crawl	*verb*	1 creep, drag, inch, slither
		2 fawn, grovel, toady
crazy	*adj*	1 foolish, idiotic, imprudent, ludicrous, mad, silly
		opposites: logical, reasonable, sensible
		2 absurd, bizarre, eccentric, peculiar, weird
		opposites: normal, regular
create	*verb*	design, develop, form, invent, make, produce, set up
		opposites: destroy, dismantle, undo
creature	*noun*	animal, beast, being, individual, person
credit	*noun*	approval, esteem, fame, glory, honour, regard, repute
		opposites: discredit, dishonour
crew	*noun*	band, company, gang, group, team
crime	*noun*	fault, misconduct, misdemeanour, offence, sin, wickedness, wrongdoing
crisp	*adj*	brittle, crumbly, fresh, snappy
		opposites: flabby, limp, vague
criticise	*verb*	bad-mouth, blame, condemn, find fault with, judge harshly
		opposites: extol, praise
crop	*noun*	harvest, produce, yield

crowd	*noun*	flock, group, herd, host, mob, multitude, pack, swarm
	verb	cluster, congregate, cram, gather, huddle, pack, swarm, throng
crude	*adj*	1 clumsy, coarse, rough, unfinished
		opposites: finished, polished
		2 indecent, obscene, rude, vulgar
		opposites: polite, refined
cruel	*adj*	brutal, cold-blooded, hard-hearted, merciless, pitiless, ruthless, vicious
		opposites: compassionate, kind, merciful
crumble	*verb*	1 break up, disintegrate, fragment
		2 collapse, deteriorate, fall apart, perish
crush	*verb*	1 compress, press, squash, squeeze
		2 conquer, defeat, overcome, subdue
	noun	crowd, huddle, jam
cry	*noun*	call, howl, scream, shriek, utterance, wail, yell
	verb	1 call, exclaim, greet, hail, scream, shout, shriek, wail, yell
		2 bawl, sob, weep, whinge
cunning	*adj*	1 crafty, devious, shifty, sneaky, tricky, wily
		opposites: frank, open, sincere
		2 clever, imaginative, sharp, shrewd, skilful
		opposites: clumsy, unskilled
cure	*verb*	heal, make well, relieve, remedy, restore
	noun	antidote, medication, remedy
curious	*adj*	1 inquisitive, prying, questioning, searching
		opposites: indifferent, uninterested
		2 extraordinary, mysterious, odd, peculiar, queer, strange, unusual
		opposites: normal, ordinary

current	*noun*	course, flow, stream
	adj	accepted, common, popular, present, prevailing, widespread
		opposites: antiquated, out of date, passé
curse	*verb*	1 blaspheme, swear
		opposites: bless, pray for
		2 condemn, put a curse on, wish evil to
curve	*noun*	arc, bend, coil, loop, turn
custom	*noun*	fashion, habit, manner, policy, style, usage, way
cut	*verb*	chop, divide, hack, pierce, sever, slit

D

damage	*noun*	destruction, harm, hurt, injury
	verb	break, disfigure, harm, hurt, injure, ruin, sabotage, spoil, wreck
		opposites: make whole, repair, restore
danger	*noun*	menace, peril, risk, threat
		opposites: safety, security
dangerous	*adj*	alarming, harmful, perilous, risky, unsafe
		opposites: harmless, safe
daring	*adj*	bold, brave, fearless, game
		opposites: afraid, fearful, timid
dark	*adj*	black, dim, dusky, gloomy
		opposites: bright, sunny
dash	*verb*	1 bound, dart, fly, hurry, race, run, rush, sprint
		opposites: dawdle, move slowly
		2 bang (against), crash, hurl, shatter, smash, throw
dawn	*noun*	beginning, daybreak, morning, start, sunrise
dazzle	*verb*	blind, confuse, overawe, sparkle
dazzling	*adj*	brilliant, glittering, radiant, shining, sparkling
		opposites: boring, dull
dead	*adj*	1 deceased, departed, lifeless
		opposites: alive, living
		2 dull, inactive, lukewarm, uninteresting, useless
		opposites: interesting, lively
deaden	*verb*	cushion, dull, lessen, muffle, soothe
		opposites: amplify, make louder
deadly	*adj*	destructive, fatal, harmful, lethal, mortal, poisonous
		opposites: healthy, life-giving

dear	*adj*	1 beloved, favourite, prized, treasured, valued
		opposites: unloved, unvalued
		2 costly, expensive, high-priced
		opposites: cheap, inexpensive, low-priced
debate	*verb*	argue, contest, discuss, dispute
		opposites: agree, cooperate
debt	*noun*	amount owing, arrears, deficit, liability, obligation
decay	*verb*	decompose, deteriorate, fade, rot, spoil, wither
		opposites: grow strong, prosper
deceive	*verb*	betray, cheat, double-cross, fool, hoodwink, mislead, swindle, trick
		opposites: enlighten, put right
decent	*adj*	1 acceptable, reasonable, satisfactory
		opposites: unacceptable, unsatisfactory
		2 considerate, generous, helpful, kind, polite, thoughtful
		opposites: bad, impolite, unkind
decide	*verb*	choose, conclude, determine, judge, make up your mind, resolve, settle
		opposites: delay, postpone, put off
declare	*verb*	announce, certify, claim, proclaim, state, testify
		opposites: conceal, keep quiet
decorate	*verb*	adorn, beautify, do up, ornament
		opposites: deface, disfigure
decrease	*verb*	abate, contract, decline, diminish, dwindle, get smaller, lessen, shrink
		opposites: get bigger, grow, increase
deed	*noun*	achievement, act, action, exploit, feat
defeat	*verb*	beat, conquer, crush, overpower, subdue, vanquish
	noun	beating, failure, reverse, setback

defend	*verb*	1 beat off, resist attack, see off
		opposite: attack
		2 guard, protect, support, uphold
		opposites: abandon, desert
definite	*adj*	certain, clear, exact, fixed, precise, settled, sure
		opposites: indefinite, vague
delay	*verb*	1 postpone, put back
		opposites: advance, bring forward
		2 hang about, hesitate, linger, loiter, wait
		opposites: hasten, hurry
deliberate	*adj*	considered, intentional, planned, prearranged
		opposites: chance, unintentional
delicate	*adj*	1 elegant, fine, flimsy, fragile, graceful, slight, subtle
		opposites: coarse, harsh, rough
		2 ailing, frail, sickly, weak
		opposites: healthy, strong, well
delicious	*adj*	delightful, enjoyable, flavoursome, luscious, tasty
		opposites: disagreeable, unpleasant
delight	*verb*	amuse, charm, entertain, make happy, please, thrill
		opposites: bore, displease, upset
deliver	*verb*	bring, carry, convey, hand over, present, transfer
		opposites: keep back, retain, return
demand	*verb*	ask for, call for, claim, insist on, request
		opposites: give up, hand over
demolish	*verb*	destroy, knock down, ruin, smash, wreck
		opposites: build, construct, erect, restore
deny	*verb*	contradict, oppose, refute, reject
		opposites: admit, agree

depart	*verb*	go, go away, leave, retire, vanish, withdraw
		opposites: arrive, come
descend	*verb*	dismount, drop, fall, go down, plunge, subside
		opposites: ascend, climb, go up
describe	*verb*	define, draw, explain, illustrate, outline, relate, report, tell
de<u>sert</u>	*noun*	solitude, void, waste, wasteland, wilderness
	adj	arid, barren, empty, infertile, uncultivated, wild
		opposites: fertile, fruitful
de<u>sert</u>	*verb*	abandon, forsake, leave, quit, renounce
deserted	*adj*	abandoned, empty, forsaken, lonely, unoccupied, vacant
		opposites: busy, crowded, full, populous, well-filled
deserve	*verb*	be worthy of, earn, merit, win
design	*noun*	1 blueprint, drawing, figure, form, model, pattern, scheme, sketch
		2 aim, goal, intent, intention, object, plan, purpose, target
desirable	*adj*	agreeable, attractive, fascinating, good, pleasing, tempting, worthwhile
		opposites: unappealing, unattractive, undesirable, unwanted
desire	*verb*	covet, hunger for, long for, request, want, wish for
		opposites: dislike, reject
despair	*noun*	depression, emptiness, gloom, hopelessness
		opposites: cheerfulness, hope
	verb	crumble, give in, give up, lose heart
desperate	*adj*	1 bold, foolhardy, hasty, rash, reckless, risky, wild
		opposites: careful, cautious, controlled

		2 dangerous, dire, drastic, hopeless, risky, serious, urgent
		opposites: hopeful, promising
despise	*verb*	detest, disdain, dislike, loathe, look down on, scorn, undervalue
		opposites: admire, appreciate, look up to
destroy	*verb*	crush, demolish, overthrow, shatter, smash, undermine
		opposites: build up, create, sustain
detail	*noun*	component, element, fact, factor, feature, ingredient, item, point
	verb	describe, enumerate, itemise, list, specify
detain	*verb*	arrest, hinder, hold, prevent, restrain, stop
		opposites: let go, release
detect	*verb*	discover, find, identify, note, notice, observe, recognise, spot, uncover
		opposites: miss, not notice, pass by, pass over
determined	*adj*	firm, insistent, persistent, purposeful, single-minded, strong-willed, stubborn
		opposites: uncertain, undecided, weak, weak-willed
detest	*verb*	dislike, hate, loathe
		opposites: admire, like, respect
develop	*verb*	1 begin, broaden, enlarge, expand, form, grow, happen, start, unfold
		opposites: contract, end, wither
		2 create, design, invent, set up
		opposites: destroy, dismantle
devoted	*adj*	caring, concerned, faithful, fond, loving, loyal, true
		opposites: indifferent, negligent, uncaring
devour	*verb*	consume, eat up, eat up greedily, swallow

die	*verb*	1 breathe one's last, expire, pass away, perish
		opposites: live, survive
		2 disappear, fade, fizzle out, peter out, wane
		opposites: flourish, grow strong
different	*adj*	changed, special, unlike, unusual
		opposites: identical, similar
difficult	*adj*	complex, complicated, demanding, hard, painful, strenuous, tough
		opposites: easy, manageable
dig	*verb*	burrow, excavate, mine, penetrate, pierce, poke, prod, tunnel
dim	*adj*	1 cloudy, dark, dull, dusky, indistinct, misty, shadowy
		opposites: bright, brilliant, clear
		2 faint, indistinct, unclear, vague, weak
		opposites: certain, clear, distinct, strong
dip	*verb*	1 dunk, immerse, plunge
		2 descend, droop, drop, fall
		opposites: ascend, rise
direct	*adj*	head-on, open, plain, point-blank, shortest, straight, uninterrupted
		opposites: crooked, indirect, roundabout
	verb	command, control, govern, guide, manage, order
directly	*adv*	at once, immediately, now
dirty	*adj*	filthy, grimy, messy, soiled, unclean
		opposites: clean, spotless
disappointed	*adj*	discouraged, dissatisfied, down-hearted, frustrated, let-down, saddened
		opposites: encouraged, hopeful, optimistic
disaster	*noun*	accident, calamity, catastrophe, misfortune, ruin, tragedy

		opposites: success, triumph
discuss	*verb*	argue, consider, debate, examine, talk about
disguise	*noun*	camouflage, deception, mask, pretence, veil
	verb	camouflage, cloak, conceal, deceive, falsify, hide, mask, screen, veil
		opposites: expose, reveal, show, uncover
disgusting	*adj*	detestable, hateful, loathsome, nasty, offensive, vile
		opposites: delightful, pleasant
dishonest	*adj*	corrupt, crooked, deceitful, false, immoral, shady
		opposites: honest, straight, trustworthy
dismiss	*verb*	banish, discharge, let go, reject, sack, spurn
		opposites: accept, appoint, take on
display	*verb*	demonstrate, exhibit, present, reveal, show
		opposites: conceal, hide
displease	*verb*	anger, annoy, infuriate, irritate, offend, upset
		opposites: delight, please
distant	*adj*	1 far, far away, far off, remote
		opposites: close, near, nearby
		2 aloof, cold, standoffish
		opposites: approachable, friendly, warm
distinct	*adj*	clear, definite, noticeable, plain, unmistakeable, well-defined
		opposites: fuzzy, ill-defined, indistinct, unclear
distress	*noun*	agony, anxiety, grief, hardship, misery, misfortune, sadness, suffering
		opposites: comfort, ease
disturb	*verb*	annoy, bother, harass, interrupt, pester, trouble, upset
		opposites: calm, put at ease, reassure
divide	*verb*	bisect, cut, distribute, separate, split
		opposites: combine, join, unite

do	*verb*	achieve, act, carry out, complete, create, effect, make, manage, perform
dodge	*verb*	avoid, evade, side-step, swerve
		opposites: approach, look out for, seek
doubtful	*adj*	1 dubious, questionable, suspect
		opposites: good, sure, trustworthy
		2 indefinite, obscure, uncertain, unclear, undecided, unsure, vague
		opposites: certain, definite
drab	*adj*	colourless, dreary, dull, gloomy, grey, shabby
		opposites: bright, colourful
drag	*verb*	draw, haul, pull, tow, tug
		opposites: push, shove, thrust
drain	*verb*	draw off, empty, exhaust, use up
		opposites: fill, fill up, replenish
	noun	channel, ditch, outlet, pipe, sewer, watercourse
draw	*verb*	1 depict, map out, outline, portray, sketch
		2 extract, pull, suck, take, tow, tug
		opposites: propel, push
		3 be equal, be even, dead-heat, tie
dreadful	*adj*	awful, ghastly, hideous, horrible, shocking, terrible
		opposites: comforting, good, pleasant
dream	*verb*	daydream, imagine, think
	noun	1 daydream, fantasy, illusion, imagination, vision
		2 ambition, desire, goal, hope, pipedream, wish
dress	*noun*	clothes, clothing, costume, garments, outfit, suit
drill	*verb*	1 coach, exercise, instruct, rehearse, teach, train
		2 bore, penetrate, pierce, puncture
drink	*verb*	drain, gulp, guzzle, sip, suck, swallow
drive	*verb*	1 direct, guide, manage, propel, push, steer, thrust

        2 coerce, compel, force, make, prod, urge

         opposites: discourage, dissuade

drop	*noun*	1	descent, fall, plunge, precipice
			opposites: ascent, rise
		2	bead, drip, droplet, sip, spot, trickle
drown	*verb*	1	deluge, engulf, flood, immerse, submerge, swamp
		2	deaden, muffle, overpower, silence, stifle, wipe out
			opposites: amplify, increase, intensify
dry	*adj*	1	arid, barren, withered, without moisture
			opposites: damp, wet
		2	boring, dreary, tiresome, uninteresting
			opposites: interesting, lively
due	*adj*	1	in arrears, outstanding, owed, owing, payable, unpaid
		2	deserved, merited, proper, right, rightful
			opposites: undeserved, inappropriate
		3	awaited, expected
			opposites: unexpected, unlooked for
dull	*adj*	1	cloudy, dim, dismal, gloomy, overcast, sunless
			opposites: bright, sunny
		2	blunt, not sharp
			opposites: keen, sharp
		3	boring, lifeless, stupid, uninteresting
			opposites: alert, exciting, interesting, stimulating
duty	*noun*	1	debt, obligation, responsibility, service, task, work
		2	levy, payment, tax
dwell	*verb*		inhabit, live, reside, stay
			opposites: leave, quit, vacate
dwindle	*verb*		decline, decrease, die out, diminish, grow smaller, lessen, tail off, waste away, wither
			opposites: grow bigger, increase, swell

E

each	*adv*	apiece, individually, per person, separately
eager	*adj*	anxious, enthusiastic, fervent, impatient, keen, zealous
		opposites: not keen, unenthusiastic
early	*adj*	1 ahead, in good time, quick, timely
		opposites: delayed, late
		2 long ago, prehistoric, primitive, young
		opposites: late, later
	adv	before, in good time, prematurely, too soon
earn	*verb*	gain, get, make, merit, obtain, receive, win
		opposites: lose, spend
earnings	*noun*	income, pay, profits, reward, salary, wages
		opposites: expenses, outgoings
ease	*noun*	comfort, enjoyment, happiness, peace, quiet, relaxation, tranquillity
		opposites: anxiety, discomfort, trouble
	verb	assist, facilitate, lighten, slide, slip, smooth
		opposites: hinder, make difficult, prevent
easy	*adj*	1 effortless, painless, simple, smooth, straightforward, undemanding
		opposites: difficult, hard, impossible
		2 carefree, comfortable, easygoing, open, serene, unworried
		opposites: anxious, troubled, worried
eat	*verb*	chew, consume, devour, feed, guzzle, munch, scoff, swallow
edge	*noun*	1 border, boundary, brim, fringe, limit, margin, rim
		opposites: centre, hub, interior, middle
		2 keenness, sharpness, urgency
		3 advantage, dominance, superiority, upper hand
		opposite: disadvantage

edible	*adj*	digestible, eatable, harmless, palatable, safe to eat, wholesome
		opposites: inedible, poisonous
educate	*verb*	civilise, coach, develop, discipline, drill, improve, instruct, school, teach, train, tutor
education	*noun*	coaching, development, discipline, guidance, improvement, instruction, teaching, training, tuition
effective	*adj*	1 able, adequate, capable, competent, efficient, useful
		opposites: inadequate, incompetent, useless
		2 convincing, forceful, impressive, persuasive, powerful, productive
		opposites: unconvincing, weak
efficient	*adj*	businesslike, competent, effective, skilful, well-organised
		opposites: clumsy, disorganised, inefficient
effort	*noun*	attempt, deed, endeavour, energy, exertion, force, strain, struggle, toil, try, work
		opposites: ease, relaxation, rest
eject	*verb*	boot out, dislodge, drive out, evict, exile, get rid of, remove, throw out
		opposites: draw in, pull in, suck in
elect	*verb*	appoint, choose, pick, select, vote for
elegant	*adj*	beautiful, delicate, fashionable, graceful, neat, refined, stylish, tasteful
		opposites: awkward, graceless, inelegant
eliminate	*verb*	annihilate, bump off, exterminate, kill, slay
		opposites: preserve, save
eloquent	*adj*	articulate, fluent, persuasive, well-spoken
		opposites: inarticulate, tongue-tied
embarrass	*verb*	disconcert, distress, fluster, shame, show up, upset
		opposites: put at ease, soothe

embarrassing	*adj*	awkward, distressing, humiliating, shameful, uncomfortable
emblem	*noun*	badge, crest, image, insignia, sign, symbol, token
embrace	*verb*	1 cuddle, enfold, hug, squeeze
		2 accept, espouse, include, involve, receive, welcome
		opposites: exclude, reject
emerge	*verb*	appear, arise, come out, crop up, develop, rise, surface, turn up
		opposites: disappear, sink
emergency	*noun*	crisis, danger, predicament
		opposite: non-emergency
emotion	*noun*	excitement, feeling, passion, sensation
emphasise	*verb*	dwell on, highlight, insist on, stress, underline
		opposites: play down, understate
employ	*verb*	engage, hire, take on
		opposites: dismiss, sack
empty	*adj*	1 bare, blank, deserted, desolate, unfilled, uninhabited, unoccupied, vacant, void
		opposites: crowded, filled, full
		2 cheap, hollow, insincere, vain, worthless
		opposites: meaningful, substantial, worthwhile
enclose	*verb*	cover, fence in, hem in, include, shut in, wrap
		opposites: exclude, reject
encourage	*verb*	aid, boost, comfort, hearten, reassure, rouse, spur, strengthen, support
		opposites: depress, discourage

end	*noun*	1 boundary, edge, extremity, limit, terminus, tip
		2 close, completion, conclusion, finale, finish, result, upshot
		opposites: beginning, outset, start
		3 aim, design, goal, objective, purpose, reason
	verb	cease, conclude, finish, stop, terminate
		opposites: begin, commence, start
endless	*adj*	boundless, continual, continuous, eternal, everlasting, infinite, uninterrupted, unlimited, whole
		opposites: brief, limited, short-lived
endure	*verb*	bear, cope with, experience, live through, put up with, tolerate
		opposites: crack under, yield to
enemy	*noun*	adversary, competitor, foe, opponent, rival
		opposites: ally, friend
energetic	*adj*	active, forceful, lively, strong, vigorous
		opposites: idle, inactive, sluggish
energy	*noun*	drive, fire, force, liveliness, power, spirit, stamina, strength, vigour, zest
engage	*verb*	appoint, employ, enlist, hire, rent, take on
		opposites: dismiss, off-load, sack
enjoy	*verb*	appreciate, delight in, like, relish, take pleasure in, use
		opposites: abhor, detest, dislike, hate
enjoyment	*noun*	delight, entertainment, fun, gaiety, happiness, joy, pleasure, satisfaction
		opposites: displeasure, dissatisfaction, unhappiness
enlarge	*verb*	develop, expand, extend, grow, inflate, lengthen, multiply, stretch, swell
		opposites: decrease, diminish, shrink
enormous	*adj*	colossal, gigantic, huge, immense, tremendous, vast
		opposites: small, tiny

enough	*adv*	adequately, moderately, passably, reasonably, satisfactorily, sufficiently
	adj	abundant, ample, plenty, sufficient
		opposites: inadequate, insufficient
enquire/inquire	*verb*	ask, question, quiz, search
enquire/inquire into	*verb*	examine, inspect, investigate, scrutinise
enrage	*verb*	anger, incense, infuriate, madden, provoke
		opposites: calm, soothe
enter into	*verb*	join, participate in, take up
		opposites: abandon, leave
entertain	*verb*	amuse, delight, please, treat
		opposites: annoy, bore, displease
enthusiasm	*noun*	fervour, great interest, keenness, passion, relish, zeal, zest
		opposites: apathy, disgust, indifference
enthusiastic	*adj*	eager, fervent, keen, passionate, wholehearted
		opposites: apathetic, reluctant, unenthusiastic
entire	*adj*	complete, continuous, full, perfect, total, unbroken, whole
		opposites: incomplete, partial
entirely	*adv*	altogether, completely, fully, perfectly, thoroughly, totally, utterly
		opposite: partly
entrance	*noun*	doorway, entry, opening
		opposites: departure, exit
environment	*noun*	background, context, habitat, scene, setting, situation, surroundings
envy	*noun*	jealousy, resentment, spite
		opposites: goodwill, tolerance

equal	*adj*	balanced, equivalent, even, even-handed, fair, just, like, matched
		opposites: unbalanced, unequal
equip	*verb*	arm, dress, fit out, prepare, provide, supply
equipment	*noun*	baggage, furnishings, gear, supplies, tackle
erect	*verb*	assemble, build, form, make, put up, set up
		opposites: destroy, pull down
error	*noun*	blunder, fault, lapse, miscalculation, mistake, oversight, slip-up
		opposite: correction
erupt	*verb*	break out, burst forth, explode, gush, spew out
escape	*verb*	1 bolt, break free, break out, evade, fly, get away, slip away
		opposites: remain, stay
		2 leak, ooze, seep, spurt, trickle
	noun	1 break-out, flight, getaway
		2 emission, leak, leakage, outflow, seepage
essential	*adj*	basic, crucial, important, necessary, needed, required, vital
		opposites: not needed, unessential
establish	*verb*	1 create, form, found, introduce, organise, set up, start
		opposites: break up, disestablish, destroy
		2 confirm, demonstrate, prove, show, verify
eternal	*adj*	ceaseless, endless, everlasting, never-ending, permanent, unending
		opposites: changeable, temporary
evade	*verb*	avoid, dodge, escape, shun, sidestep, steer clear of
		opposites: approach, face, meet
evaporate	*verb*	disappear, disperse, dry, fade, melt away, vanish

even	*adj*	1 balanced, equal, level, matching, well-balanced
		opposites: ill-matched, odd, unequal
		2 flat, parallel, regular, rhythmical, smooth
		opposites: irregular, uneven
event	*noun*	happening, incident, occasion, occurrence, possibility
eventually	*adv*	at last, finally, in due time, ultimately
everlasting	*adj*	ceaseless, endless, eternal, never-ending, unceasing
		opposites: fleeting, short-lived, temporary
evil	*adj*	bad, devilish, immoral, malevolent, vicious, vile, wicked
		opposites: angelic, good
exact	*adj*	accurate, identical, precise, true
		opposites: approximate, inexact
exaggerate	*verb*	emphasise, enlarge, magnify, overestimate, overstate
		opposites: belittle, play down, understate
examine	*verb*	check, consider, explore, inspect, investigate, question, study, test
example	*noun*	case, illustration, instance, model, occurrence, sample, type
excel	*verb*	do better than, outclass, outshine, overshadow, surpass
		opposites: be inferior, do badly, fail
excellent	*adj*	admirable, first-class, great, notable, outstanding, remarkable, splendid, superb, unequalled, wonderful
		opposites: inferior, poor, undistinguished
exceptional	*adj*	extraordinary, notable, outstanding, rare, special, unequalled
		opposites: mediocre, ordinary, unexceptional

excess   *noun*   overabundance, overflow, overload, surplus
                                opposites: dearth, lack of

excite   *verb*   arouse, inflame, inspire, rouse, stir up, thrill
                                opposites: bore, calm, pacify

exclaim   *verb*   blurt, call, cry, cry out, shout, utter

exclude   *verb*   ban, bar, eject, evict, keep out, leave out, omit, reject, remove, shut out
                                opposites: admit, allow, include

excuse   *verb*   explain, forgive, justify, let off, overlook, pardon
(rhymes with 'lose')   *opposites:* accuse, blame, condemn

excuse   *noun*   alibi, defence, explanation, plea, reason
(rhymes with 'loose')

exercise   *verb*   drill, practise, train, work out

                        noun   aerobics, drill, exertion, practice, toil, training, work, workout

exhausted   *adj*   all in, done in, drained, empty, tired out, weak, worn out
                                opposites: energetic, fresh, lively, vigorous

exist   *verb*   live, survive
                                opposites: die out, pass away

exit   *noun*   departure point, outlet, way out
                                opposites: entrance, way in

expand   *verb*   1 blow up, enlarge, fill out, grow, increase, inflate, open, spread, swell
                                opposites: contract, decrease, diminish

                                2 branch out, develop, extend, grow larger

expect   *verb*   anticipate, count on, foresee, hope for, look for, look forward to, rely on

expel   *verb*   banish, cast out, discharge, drive out, eject, evict, exclude, remove, throw out
                                opposites: admit, bring in, welcome

expense	*noun*	charge, cost, expenditure, outlay, payment
expensive	*adj*	costly, dear, exorbitant, overpriced
		opposites: cheap, inexpensive, underpriced
experience	*noun*	know-how, knowledge, practice, training, understanding
		opposites: immaturity, inexperience
expert	*noun*	master, professional, specialist
		opposites: amateur, beginner, novice
	adj	clever, handy, knowledgeable, master, professional, skilful, skilled
		opposites: amateur, inexpert, unskilled
explain	*verb*	account for, clarify, clear up, define, demonstrate, describe, justify, solve, spell out
		opposites: leave unclear, obscure
explore	*verb*	1 analyse, examine, inspect, investigate, probe
		2 search, survey, tour, travel, voyage
expose	*verb*	bring to light, disclose, display, divulge, exhibit, reveal, show, uncover, unveil
		opposites: conceal, cover, hide
express	*verb*	disclose, pronounce, put into words, say, speak, state, tell
		opposites: conceal, suppress, withhold
expression	*noun*	1 declaration, language, phrase, statement, utterance, word
		2 aspect, indication, look, show, sign
exquisite	*adj*	admirable, attractive, beautiful, delicate, elegant, lovely, refined, superb
		opposites: flawed, imperfect, poor, ugly

extend	*verb*	1 give, hold out, offer, present, reach out, stretch
		opposites: draw back, keep back
		2 develop, draw out, enlarge, expand, increase, lengthen, unfold, unroll, widen
		opposites: decrease, shorten, roll up
exterior	*noun*	covering, façade, face, finish, outside, shell, skin, surface
		opposites: inside, interior
extra	*adj*	added, additional, excess, inessential, more, needless, supplementary
		opposites: basic, essential, necessary
extraordinary	*adj*	amazing, exceptional, outstanding, phenomenal, rare, remarkable, special, strange, surprising, uncommon, weird, wonderful
		opposites: commonplace, ordinary, unremarkable
extravagant	*adj*	lavish, reckless, showy, wasteful
		opposites: careful, mean, thrifty
extreme	*adj*	1 farthest, last, outermost, remotest
		opposites: near, nearest
		2 greatest, high, highest, maximum, utter, utmost
		opposites: least, little
extremely	*adv*	exceptionally, excessively, greatly, highly, intensively, unusually, utterly, very
		opposites: moderately, slightly

F

fabulous	*adj*	1 imaginary, legendary, mythical, unreal
		opposites: actual, real
		2 amazing, breathtaking, marvellous, spectacular, wonderful
		opposites: commonplace, ordinary
face	*noun*	1 countenance, expression, features, look
		2 cover, exterior, façade, front, surface
		opposites: back, interior, underneath
	verb	confront, cope with, deal with, meet, oppose, tackle
		opposites: avoid, evade
fact	*noun*	circumstance, deed, detail, event, happening, incident, item, occurrence, truth
		opposites: fiction, lie
fade	*verb*	die (away), dim, diminish, disappear, dwindle, fail, vanish, wane, wither
		opposites: flourish, grow strong
fail	*verb*	decline, dwindle, founder, go under, sink, weaken
		opposites: improve, prosper, succeed
faint	*adj*	dim, dull, faded, feeble, hazy, indistinct, slight, soft, weak
		opposites: clear, distinct, strong
fair	*adj*	1 bright, clear, fine, sunny, unclouded
		opposites: cloudy, dull
		2 blond, fair-haired, flaxen, light-coloured
		opposite: dark
		3 adequate, average, equal, middling, moderate, passable, reasonable, satisfactory
		opposites: excessive, extreme
		4 honest, impartial, just, trustworthy, unbiased
		opposites: biased, dishonest, unjust, untrustworthy

faith	*noun*	1 belief, creed, religion
		2 confidence, loyalty, promise, sincerity, trust, truth
faithful	*adj*	1 accurate, exact, strict, true
		opposites: inaccurate, inexact
		2 dependable, loyal, reliable, staunch
		opposites: disloyal, treacherous, untrustworthy
fake	*noun*	copy, forgery, fraud, hoax, imitation
		opposites: original, real thing
fall	*verb*	1 descend, drop, go down, plunge, sink, tumble
		opposites: go up, rise
		2 collapse, crash, diminish, dwindle, lessen, yield
		opposites: grow, improve, succeed
false	*adj*	1 artificial, bogus, counterfeit, fake, sham
		opposites: genuine, real
		2 incorrect, mistaken, untrue, wrong
		opposites: correct, truthful
		3 disloyal, hypocritical, treacherous, unreliable, untrustworthy
		opposites: loyal, true
fame	*noun*	celebrity, glory, honour, renown, stardom
		opposite: obscurity
familiar	*adj*	1 common, everyday, ordinary, routine
		opposites: bizarre, uncommon, unusual
		2 close, friendly, intimate, sociable
		opposites: formal, reserved, standoffish
famine	*noun*	dearth, hunger, scarcity, starvation
		opposite: plenty
famous	*adj*	celebrated, eminent, famed, great, honoured, notable, renowned, well-known
		opposites: anonymous, unknown

fancy	*adj*	decorative, elegant, gaudy, ornamental, ornamented
		opposites: plain, ordinary, unadorned
fantastic	*adj*	1 extraordinary, great, marvellous, sensational, spectacular, wonderful
		opposites: humdrum, ordinary, unspectacular
		2 eccentric, grotesque, outlandish, peculiar, ridiculous, weird
		opposites: plain, ordinary, run-of-the-mill
farewell	*noun*	adieu, departure, goodbye, parting, send-off
		opposites: greeting, meeting
fascinating	*adj*	bewitching, charming, interesting, intriguing
		opposites: boring, dull, uninteresting
fast	*adj*	brisk, hasty, hurried, quick, rapid, swift
		opposites: leisurely, slow, unhurried
	verb	abstain, diet, go hungry, not eat, starve
		opposites: eat, gorge
fasten	*verb*	attach, chain, clamp, connect, fix, grip, join, link, tie, unite
		opposites: disconnect, unfasten, untie
fat	*adj*	obese, overweight, plump, stout
		opposites: slim, thin
fatal	*adj*	deadly, final, lethal, mortal, terminal
		opposites: harmless, non-fatal
fault	*noun*	1 blemish, defect, error, failing, flaw, lapse, mistake, slip
		2 offence, shortcoming, sin, transgression, wrong
favour	*noun*	benefit, courtesy, gift, present, support
favourable	*adj*	advantageous, agreeable, beneficial, encouraging, helpful, promising, suitable, welcoming
		opposites: discouraging, unfavourable

fear	*noun*	alarm, anxiety, concern, distress, dread, fright, panic, terror, unease, worry
		opposites: fearlessness, unconcern
fearless	*adj*	brave, courageous, daring, unafraid
		opposites: afraid, frightened, timid
feast	*noun*	celebration, dinner, entertainment, treat
feat	*noun*	achievement, attainment, deed, exploit, performance
feature	*noun*	aspect, attribute, facet, factor, highlight, item, quality
features	*noun*	countenance, face, looks
feeble	*adj*	delicate, exhausted, frail, indecisive, ineffective, poor, slight, timid, weak
		opposites: effective, strong, tough
feed	*verb*	1 nourish, provide for, strengthen, supply
		2 dine, eat
feel	*verb*	1 caress, fondle, handle, hold, stroke, touch
		2 believe, consider, judge, seem, sense, think
		3 enjoy, suffer
feelings	*noun*	affections, emotions, passions, self-esteem, sensitivity
feminine	*adj*	delicate, gentle, graceful, ladylike, soft, tender, womanly
		opposite: masculine
fence	*noun*	barricade, barrier, guard, paling, railings
ferocious	*adj*	brutal, fearsome, fierce, merciless, ruthless, savage, vicious, violent, wild
		opposites: gentle, mild-mannered
fertile	*adj*	abundant, flowering, fruit-bearing, lush, luxuriant, plentiful, productive, rich
		opposites: arid, barren, unproductive
festival	*noun*	anniversary, carnival, celebration, gala, holiday, holy day, jubilee

feud   *noun*   bitter argument, conflict, discord, enmity, hostility,
                             ill will, quarrel, rivalry, vendetta
                             opposites: agreement, peace

few   *adj*   inadequate, infrequent, in short supply, insufficient,
                             not many, rare, scarce
                             opposites: great deal, many

fickle   *adj*   changeable, disloyal, treacherous, unfaithful,
                             unreliable, variable
                             opposites: dependable, reliable

field   *noun*   grassland, green, land, lawn, meadow, pasture,
                             pitch, playing field

fierce   *adj*   fearsome, ferocious, furious, threatening, vicious,
                             violent, wild
                             opposites: calm, gentle, kind, tender-hearted

fight   *verb*   battle, brawl, clash, dispute, oppose, quarrel,
                             squabble, wrestle

                    noun   argument, battle, brawl, clash, contest, duel, quarrel,
                             riot, war

figure   *noun*   1 body, form, frame, physique, shape, silhouette,
                             torso

                             2 amount, digit, number, numeral, price, sum, value

                             3 design, device, diagram, emblem, image, outline,
                             shape, sign, sketch, symbol

film   *noun*   1 coat, coating, covering, glaze, layer, sheet, skin,
                             veil

                             2 documentary, feature film, motion picture, movie,
                             video

final   *adj*   concluding, decisive, end, last, latest, ultimate
                             opposites: early, first

finally   *adv*   at last, completely, definitely, eventually, for ever, in
                             conclusion, lastly, permanently, ultimately
                             opposites: firstly, to begin with

find	*verb*	come across, detect, discover, experience, learn, locate, observe, obtain, recover, regain, track down, turn up, uncover
		opposites: lose, miss
fine	*adj*	1 admirable, attractive, beautiful, excellent, good, handsome, splendid, superior
		opposites: ordinary, poor, unattractive
		2 dainty, delicate, flimsy, fragile, light, slender, thin
		opposites: coarse, thick
		3 cloudless, fair, pleasant, sunny
		opposites: cloudy, overcast
finish	*verb*	achieve, close, complete, conclude, end, finalise, settle, stop, terminate
		opposites: begin, commence, start
firm	*adj*	definite, fixed, rigid, secure, stable, stiff, strong, sturdy, unyielding
		opposites: insecure, moveable, soft, yielding
first	*adj*	1 basic, chief, fundamental, primary, principal
		opposite: secondary
		2 earliest, foremost, initial, introductory, opening, original
		opposites: last, latest
fit	*verb*	adapt, adjust, arrange, join, match, modify, place, position, shape, suit
	noun	attack, convulsion, outburst, seizure, spasm
fix	*verb*	1 adhere, attach, bind, connect, fasten, glue, nail, pin, place, secure, stick, tie
		opposites: loosen, separate, untie
		2 correct, mend, rearrange, repair, restore, sort
		opposites: break, destroy
		3 arrange, confirm, decide, establish, influence
		opposites: dismantle, dissolve

flair	*noun*	aptitude, genius, gift, knack, skill, style, talent
flash	*verb*	1 blaze, flare, flicker, gleam, glitter, shimmer, sparkle, twinkle
		2 bolt, dart, race, shoot, speed, sprint
flat	*adj*	1 even, horizontal, level, smooth, uniform
		opposites: uneven, vertical
		2 bored, boring, depressed, dull, empty, lifeless, stale, uninteresting
		opposites: excited, interesting, lively
flavour	*noun*	aroma, essence, odour, quality, relish, style, tang, taste
flaw	*noun*	blemish, defect, failing, fault, imperfection, mistake, shortcoming
flawless	*adj*	faultless, impeccable, perfect, unblemished, undamaged, whole
		opposites: damaged, faulty, imperfect
flexible	*adj*	1 double-jointed, elastic, lithe, loose-limbed, pliable, springy, supple
		opposites: stiff, unyielding
		2 accommodating, adaptable, open, responsive
		opposites: inflexible, stubborn, unresponsive
flick	*verb*	flip, hit lightly, jab, rap, strike lightly, tap, touch, whip
flicker	*verb*	flash, glitter, shimmer, sparkle, twinkle
		opposites: gleam, shine
flight	*noun*	1 air travel, aviation, soaring
		2 break-away, escape, exit, getaway, retreat
fling	*verb*	hurl, let fly, lob, pitch, propel, shoot, sling, throw, toss
float	*verb*	bob, drift, hover, sail, slide, swim
		opposite: sink
flood	*verb*	drown, engulf, fill, flow, overflow, pour, soak, submerge, swamp

flourish	*verb*	bloom, blossom, develop, flower, grow, increase, succeed, thrive
		opposites: fail, wilt, wither
flow	*verb*	cascade, glide, gush, pour, spurt, stream, surge, swirl
fly	*verb*	1 dart, dash, flit, glide, hover, soar, take wing
		2 escape, get away, retreat, run for it
foggy	*adj*	confused, dark, dim, grey, hazy, misty, murky, unclear
		opposite: clear
follow	*verb*	1 come after, come next, go after, shadow, track, trail
		opposites: lead, show the way
		2 imitate, live up to, obey, support
		opposites: abandon, break away from, desert
		3 catch on, comprehend, grasp, note, observe, see, understand
		opposites: fail to see, miss
fond	*adj*	affectionate, caring, devoted, doting, loving, tender
		opposites: hostile, unloving
food	*noun*	diet, nourishment, provisions, rations, refreshment
fool	*noun*	ass, blockhead, clown, dunderhead, dupe, idiot, imbecile, simpleton
	verb	con, deceive, dupe, hoax, hoodwink, mislead, swindle, trick
fool around	*verb*	be silly, clown, jest, mess about, play the fool, tease
forbid	*verb*	ban, deny, exclude, hinder, outlaw, prevent, prohibit, refuse, veto
		opposites: allow, permit
force	*verb*	compel, make, oblige, pressurise, push, thrust, urge
		opposites: beg, persuade
	noun	compulsion, duress, influence, might, power, strength, violence

forecast	*verb*	estimate, expect, foresee, foretell, predict, prophesy
foreign	*adj*	alien, distant, strange, unfamiliar, unknown, unrelated
		opposites: familiar, native
forget	*verb*	lose sight of, neglect, not to remember, omit, overlook, think no more of
		opposites: bear in mind, recall, remember
forgive	*verb*	absolve, condone, excuse, exonerate, let off, overlook, pardon
		opposites: blame, censure
form	*noun*	1 appearance, body, build, figure, outline, shape, structure
		2 document, paper, plan, questionnaire, schedule
former	*adj*	earlier, foregoing, long ago, old, previous, prior, sometime
		opposites: current, latter, present, subsequent
fortunate	*adj*	favourable, favoured, helpful, lucky, profitable, promising, prosperous, successful
		opposites: ill-fated, unfortunate, unlucky
foundation	*noun*	base, bottom, groundwork, substance, underpinning
fracture	*noun*	break, crack, fissure, gap, opening, rupture, split
fragile	*adj*	breakable, brittle, delicate, fine, flimsy, insubstantial
		opposites: durable, tough, unbreakable
fragment	*noun*	bit, chip, fraction, part, piece, remnant, scrap, shred, sliver
		opposites: total, whole
frame	*noun*	body, bodywork, build, chassis, form, framework, shell, structure
frantic	*adj*	desperate, frenzied, furious, hectic, raving, wild
		opposites: calm, composed
free	*adj*	1 free-of-charge, without charge
		opposites: costly, paid

2 able (to), allowed, available, permitted, willing
opposites: prevented (from), unable (to)

3 liberated, unforced, unobstructed, unoccupied, unrestrained, unused
opposites: forced, kept in check, occupied

frequent   *adj*   customary, everyday, habitual, incessant, numerous, regular, repeated, usual
opposites: infrequent, occasional, rare

fresh   *adj*   1 bright, brisk, clear, energetic, glowing, healthy, lively, refreshed, refreshing, sparkling, wholesome
opposites: dull, tasteless

2 additional, different, extra, further, more

3 green, new, raw, recent, unspoilt, young, youthful
opposites: jaded, old, overripe

friendly   *adj*   affectionate, close, companionable, familiar, favourable, good, helpful, intimate, neighbourly, outgoing, sociable, welcoming
opposites: cold, hostile, unfriendly, unsociable

frighten   *verb*   alarm, intimidate, petrify, scare, terrify, terrorise
opposites: calm, reassure

front   *noun*   1 beginning, forefront, head, lead
opposites: back, rear

2 exterior, façade, face, facing
opposites: interior, underlying structure

fruitful   *adj*   abundant, fertile, plentiful, productive, profitable, rewarding, rich, successful, useful, worthwhile
opposites: barren, fruitless, ineffective

fulfil   *verb*   accomplish, achieve, carry out, complete, conclude, effect, finish, obey, perform, realise, satisfy
opposites: break, fail

full	*adj*	abundant, ample, brimful, complete, comprehensive, entire, generous, maximum, plentiful, sufficient, thorough
		opposites: incomplete, insufficient, partial
fun	*noun*	amusement, enjoyment, entertainment, joking, joy, merriment, play, pleasure
funny	*adj*	1 amusing, comical, entertaining, hilarious, humorous, jocular, witty
		opposites: boring, dull, solemn, unfunny
		2 mysterious, odd, puzzling, queer, strange, suspicious, unusual
		opposites: normal, open, plain
furious	*adj*	1 angry, enraged, fuming, incensed, livid, mad, raging, savage
		opposites: calm, composed
		2 frenzied, stormy, tempestuous, turbulent, violent, wild
		opposites: calm, mild, still
fury	*noun*	anger, ferocity, frenzy, madness, passion, rage, savagery, violence, wrath
		opposites: calm, composure
fuss	*noun*	bother, commotion, excitement, flap, flurry, hurry, trouble, worry
		opposites: calm, peace
futile	*adj*	fruitless, hollow, ineffectual, pointless, unsuccessful, useless, worthless
		opposites: fruitful, profitable, useful

G

gadget	*noun*	appliance, contraption, device, invention, tool
gag	*verb*	choke, muzzle, silence, stifle, suppress, throttle
gain	*verb*	achieve, acquire, attain, earn, gather, get, increase, obtain, procure, profit, realise, secure, win
		opposites: fail to achieve, lose
gallop	*verb*	bolt, dart, dash, hasten, hurry, race, run, rush, speed, sprint
gamble	*verb*	bet, chance, have a flutter, risk, speculate, stake, take a chance, wager
game	*noun*	1 amusement, entertainment, pastime, play, recreation, sport
		opposites: employment, work
		2 wild animals (hunted for meat)
gang	*noun*	band, club, company, crew, crowd, group, pack, set, squad, team
gaol/jail	*noun*	dungeon, prison, penitentiary
garments	*noun*	clothes, clothing, costume, dress, outfit, robes, uniform, vestments
gasp	*verb*	blow, breathe hard, choke, gulp, pant, puff
gather	*verb*	1 assemble, build up, collect, group, heap, muster, pile up, select
		opposites: disperse, scatter, spread
		2 assume, conclude, infer, learn, understand
gathering	*noun*	assembly, company, congregation, crowd, flock, group, meeting, throng
gaunt	*adj*	bony, emaciated, haggard, pinched, scraggy, skinny
		opposites: fat, plump
gay	*adj*	1 bright, brilliant, festive, gaudy, showy, sparkling
		opposites: dull, dreary
		2 cheerful, glad, happy, lively, merry, vivacious
		opposites: gloomy, sad

gaze   *verb*   gape, look, regard, stare, view, watch
                           opposites: glance, glimpse

gem   *noun*   1 jewel, pearl, precious stone
                           2 masterpiece, prize, treasure

general   *adj*   common, customary, everyday, normal, ordinary,
                           popular, public, regular, typical, usual
                           opposites: particular, special, unusual

generous   *adj*   1 benevolent, charitable, hospitable, kind,
                              magnanimous, soft-hearted, unselfish
                              opposites: mean, selfish

                           2 ample, lavish, overflowing, plentiful
                              opposites: inadequate, mean, small, tiny

gentle   *adj*   humane, kind, kindly, merciful, mild, peaceful,
                           quiet, smooth, sweet-tempered, tender
                           opposites: crude, hard, harsh, unkind

genuine   *adj*   1 authentic, legitimate, pure, real, sound, true
                              opposites: artificial, false, sham

                           2 frank, honest, sincere, unaffected
                              opposites: dishonest, insincere

germinate   *verb*   bud, develop, grow, shoot up, sprout
                           opposites: die, wither

gesture   *noun*   act, indication, motion, sign, signal, wave

get   *verb*   achieve, acquire, become, catch, come by, come
                           down with, contract, earn, fetch, gain, grab, inherit,
                           make, manage, move, obtain, pick up, receive,
                           secure, seize, take, win
                           opposite: lose

ghost   *noun*   apparition, hallucination, image, phantom, spirit, spook

giant   *adj*   colossal, enormous, gigantic, huge, immense,
                           king-size, large, prodigious, vast
                           opposites: dwarf, puny, small, tiny

gift	*noun*	1 bequest, donation, grant, legacy, offering, present
		2 ability, aptitude, flair, genius, knack, power, talent
gigantic	*adj*	colossal, enormous, huge, immense, stupendous, vast
		opposites: small, tiny
giggle	*verb*	chortle, chuckle, laugh, snigger, titter
give	*verb*	allow, award, concede, contribute, deliver, grant, hand over, offer, pay, permit, present, produce, provide, supply, surrender, yield
		opposites: take, recover, retrieve
glad	*adj*	cheerful, cheery, delighted, happy, joyful, merry, overjoyed, pleased
		opposites: downhearted, miserable, sad
glamorous	*adj*	attractive, dazzling, elegant, exciting, fascinating, glittering, smart
		opposites: drab, dull, inelegant
glance	*verb*	1 glimpse, look, peek, peep, scan, view
		opposites: gaze, stare, watch
		2 brush, ricochet, skim, touch lightly
glare	*verb*	1 blaze, dazzle, flare, shine
		2 frown, glower, look daggers at, scowl
		opposite: smile
gleam	*verb*	flicker, glimmer, glint, glisten, glitter, shimmer, shine, sparkle
gleaming	*adj*	bright, brilliant, glistening, glowing, polished, shining
		opposites: dull, unpolished
glimpse	*noun*	glance, look, peek, peep, sight
		opposites: long look, stare
glitter	*verb*	flash, gleam, glint, glisten, scintillate, shimmer, shine, sparkle, twinkle

gloomy	*adj*	dark, depressing, dismal, dreary, dull, miserable, sad
		opposites: bright, cheerful, happy
glorious	*adj*	brilliant, illustrious, magnificent, marvellous, splendid, triumphant
		opposites: dreadful, inglorious, shameful
glossy	*adj*	bright, brilliant, polished, shining, shiny, sleek, smooth
		opposites: dull, unpolished
glowing	*adj*	beaming, bright, flushed, luminous, ruddy, vivid, warm
		opposite: dull
go	*verb*	advance, depart, journey, make for, move, proceed, progress, reach, travel, walk
		opposites: remain, stay
go ahead	*verb*	advance, begin, continue, proceed
go away	*verb*	depart, disappear, exit, leave, retreat, vanish, withdraw
go back	*verb*	desert, forsake, retreat, return
go by	*verb*	1 elapse, flow, pass
		2 follow, heed, observe
go into	*verb*	analyse, consider, delve into, examine, investigate, study, undertake
go over	*verb*	examine, inspect, read, recall, review, revise, study
go under	*verb*	collapse, die, drown, fail
go with	*verb*	1 accompany, escort, join
		2 agree, blend, complement, correspond with, match, partner, suit
goal	*noun*	aim, destination, destiny, end, intention, limit, mark, objective, purpose, target
good	*adj*	1 admirable, charitable, considerate, dependable, excellent, honourable, kind, moral, noble,

praiseworthy, true, trustworthy, upright, virtuous, worthy

opposites: bad, evil, immoral

2 acceptable, adequate, competent, efficient, favourable, genuine, helpful, nourishing, pleasing, reliable, right, satisfactory, skilful, thorough, useful, valuable

opposites: inefficient, poor, unhelpful, useless

gorgeous	*adj*	attractive, beautiful, glamorous, good-looking, lovely, splendid, stunning
		opposites: drab, plain, unattractive
govern	*verb*	command, control, manage, order, oversee, rule, supervise
		opposites: obey, serve
grab	*verb*	capture, catch, clutch, grasp, grip, seize, snatch
		opposites: let go, release
graceful	*adj*	elegant, flowing, natural, pleasing, smooth, supple
		opposites: clumsy, graceless, inelegant
gracious	*adj*	charitable, considerate, friendly, hospitable, kind, merciful, polite, well-mannered
		opposites: disobliging, impolite, nasty, ungracious
gradual	*adj*	even, gentle, leisurely, moderate, piecemeal, regular, slow, steady, unhurried
		opposites: abrupt, irregular, sudden
grasp	*verb*	1 catch, clasp, clutch, grab, grip, hold, seize, snatch
		opposites: let go, release
		2 comprehend, follow, realise, see, understand
		opposites: be confused, fail to understand
grateful	*adj*	appreciative, obliged, thankful
		opposite: ungrateful

great	*adj*	1 big, bulky, colossal, enormous, gigantic, heavy, huge, immense, large, tremendous, vast *opposites:* little, small
		2 admirable, excellent, good, magnanimous, noble, wonderful *opposites:* bad, contemptible, paltry
		3 famous, illustrious, important, impressive, remarkable, skilful, skilled, talented, valuable *opposites:* insignificant, of no account, unimportant
green	*adj*	emerald, jade, lime green, olive, pea green
grief	*noun*	anguish, bereavement, distress, heartache, heartbreak, misery, mourning, sadness, sorrow, suffering, trouble *opposites:* contentment, delight, happiness, joy
grip	*verb*	catch, clasp, clutch, grasp, hold, seize, snatch *opposites:* free, let go, release, unclasp
groan	*verb*	complain, cry, lament, moan, sigh, sob, wail *opposites:* applaud, commend, praise
groove	*noun*	canal, channel, cut, furrow, trench
ground	*noun*	1 arena, field, park, pitch, stadium
		2 dirt, earth, land, soil, turf
group	*noun*	1 band, batch, clutch, collection, congregation, crowd, pack, set, team *opposites:* individual, member, unit
		2 assortment, category, class, classification, family, genus, order, organisation, species
grow	*verb*	1 breed, evolve, flourish, flower, ripen, rise, shoot, sprout *opposites:* die, wither
		2 become, broaden, develop, expand, improve, increase, multiply, progress, succeed, swell,

thicken, widen

opposites: decline, decrease, fail

grumble   *verb*   bleat, complain, gripe, grouse, murmur, mutter, whine

opposites: applaud, commend, praise

guarantee   *verb*   certify, ensure, make sure of, pledge, promise, vouch for

guide   *verb*   1 escort, head, lead, pilot, shepherd, steer, usher

opposites: misdirect, mislead

2 command, control, direct, educate, influence, instruct, manage, rule, supervise, teach, train

opposites: follow, obey

guilt   *noun*   blame, disgrace, regret, remorse, shame, sinfulness, wickedness, wrong

opposites: blamelessness, innocence

gust   *noun*   blast, breeze, flurry, gale, puff, squall, wind

H

habit	*noun*	custom, inclination, manner, mannerism, nature, practice, rule, tendency, way
habitual	*adj*	accustomed, customary, natural, persistent, regular, usual
		opposites: occasional, uncommon
haggle	*verb*	bargain, barter, dispute, squabble, wrangle
		opposites: accept, agree
halt	*verb*	call it a day, end, pack it in, quit, stop
		opposites: continue, go on
hammer	*verb*	bang, beat, drive, hit, knock
hamper	*verb*	cramp, frustrate, hamstring, hinder, hold up, interfere with, obstruct
		opposites: aid, help
hand down	*verb*	give, grant, pass on, transfer, will
hand out	*verb*	dish out, distribute, give out, share out
hand over	*verb*	deliver, donate, give, present, release, surrender, yield
handle	*verb*	feel, finger, fondle, grasp, hold, manipulate, operate, touch, use
handsome	*adj*	attractive, elegant, good-looking
		opposites: plain, ugly
handy	*adj*	1 available, close, near, nearby, ready
		opposites: not at hand, unavailable
		2 convenient, helpful, practical, serviceable, skilful, useful
		opposites: unhelpful, useless
hang	*verb*	1 dangle, drop, droop, hover, sag, suspend, swing
		2 attach, fasten, fix, stick
haphazard	*adj*	aimless, careless, disorganised, hit-or-miss, random, slapdash, unmethodical
		opposites: deliberate, planned

happen *verb* arise, come about, crop up, develop, follow, occur, result, transpire

happy *adj* cheerful, contented, delighted, glad, jolly, joyous, merry, thrilled

opposites: miserable, sad, unhappy

harass *verb* annoy, bother, disturb, hound, pester, torment, trouble, worry

opposites: assist, help

hard *adj* 1 firm, solid, stiff, tough, unyielding

opposites: plastic, soft, yielding

2 cruel, fierce, hard-hearted, pitiless, ruthless, strict, stubborn, unfeeling

opposites: gentle, mild, sensitive

3 difficult, not easy

opposites: easy, simple

hardly *adv* barely, faintly, infrequently, only, only just, scarcely, with difficulty

opposites: comfortably, easily, very

hardship *noun* adversity, difficulty, misfortune, persecution, suffering, trouble

opposite: ease

hardy *adj* fit, healthy, lusty, robust, strong, tough

opposites: unhealthy, weak

harm *verb* abuse, damage, hurt, ill-treat, injure, maim, ruin, spoil, wound

opposites: assist, benefit, protect

harmless *adj* gentle, innocent, inoffensive

opposites: destructive, evil, hurtful

harsh *adj* 1 abrasive, coarse, crude, grating, jarring, rasping, rough

opposites: pleasing, smooth

2 bitter, brutal, cruel, grim, pitiless, ruthless, severe, stern

opposites: gentle, merciful, mild

harvest *noun* crop, produce, result, return

verb acquire, collect, gather, pick, pluck, reap

opposites: plant, sow

hassle *noun* bother, difficulty, fight, problem, quarrel, squabble, trouble

opposites: agreement, friendliness, peace

hasty *adj* 1 brief, fast, fleeting, hurried, prompt, rapid, short, snappy, swift

opposite: slow

2 foolhardy, heedless, hot-headed, hot-tempered, quick-tempered, reckless, thoughtless

opposites: careful, cautious, deliberate, even-tempered

hate *verb* abhor, despise, detest, dislike, loathe

opposites: like, love

hateful *adj* abominable, despicable, horrible, loathsome, repulsive, revolting, vile

opposites: likeable, loveable

hazy *adj* cloudy, foggy, fuzzy, indistinct, misty, obscure, overcast, unclear, vague

opposites: clear, definite

head *noun* 1 brain, intellect, intelligence, mind, skull

2 boss, chief, commander, director, leader, manager, principal

opposite: underling

headstrong	*adj*	foolhardy, heedless, impulsive, obstinate, rash, reckless, stubborn, unruly
		opposites: accommodating, careful, cautious
heal	*verb*	cure, mend, remedy, restore, settle, treat
healthy	*adj*	blooming, fit, flourishing, physically fit, robust, strong, sturdy, vigorous, well
		opposites: ill, unfit, unwell, weak
heap	*noun*	collection, hoard, mass, mountain, pile, stack, store
	verb	build, collect, gather, hoard, increase, lavish, pile, shower, stack, stockpile
hear	*verb*	catch, discover, eavesdrop, heed, learn, listen, overhear
heart	*noun*	1 centre, core, crux, essence, hub, kernel, middle, nub, nucleus, pith
		opposites: exterior, margin, outside
		2 bravery, character, courage, spirit, will
		opposites: dispiritedness, weakness
		3 affection, compassion, feeling, humanity, love, soul, sympathy, tenderness, understanding
		opposites: inhumanity, lack of feeling
heartless	*adj*	brutal, cold, cold-hearted, cruel, inhuman, merciless, pitiless, stern, unfeeling, unkind
		opposites: considerate, kind, sympathetic
hearty	*adj*	enthusiastic, jovial, sincere, warm, wholehearted
		opposites: cold, half-hearted
heat	*verb*	inflame, toast, warm up
		opposites: chill, cool
heavy	*adj*	1 laden, leaden, massive, weighty
		opposites: airy, light
		2 depressed, dull, sluggish, stodgy
		opposites: alert, bright, energetic
		3 considerable, excessive, onerous, severe
		opposites: light, slight

hectic	*adj*	chaotic, exciting, fast, furious, rapid, turbulent, wild *opposites:* leisurely, unexciting
heed	*verb*	attend, consider, follow, listen, mark, note, obey, observe, regard, take notice of *opposites:* disregard, ignore
help	*verb*	aid, befriend, ease, improve, relieve, remedy, restore, serve, stand by, support *opposites:* abandon, hinder, oppose
helpful	*adj*	caring, considerate, co-operative, friendly, kind, neighbourly, sympathetic, useful *opposites:* unhelpful, useless, worthless
hesitate	*verb*	dither, falter, halt, pause, shrink (from), waver *opposites:* be decisive, charge ahead, go for it
hide	*verb*	bury, conceal, cover, disguise, screen, shelter, withhold *opposites:* display, reveal, show
hideous	*adj*	awful, disgusting, gruesome, horrendous, horrible, loathsome, revolting, ugly *opposites:* appealing, attractive, beautiful
high	*adj*	1 elevated, lofty, prominent, steep, tall, towering *opposites:* flat, low 2 distinguished, eminent, extraordinary, extreme, great, important, lavish, superior *opposites:* undistinguished, plain, unimportant 3 acute, high-pitched, penetrating, piercing, shrill *opposites:* deep, low, low-pitched
hilarious	*adj*	amusing, comical, funny, hysterical, merry *opposites:* grave, serious
hinder	*verb*	deter, hamper, hold back, impede, obstruct, oppose, prevent, stop, thwart *opposites:* assist, help

hint	*verb*	imply, indicate, insinuate, mention, suggest
		opposites: assert, state
hit	*verb*	bang, beat, bump, clip, collide with, cuff, knock, punch, slap, smack, strike, wallop, whack
hoarse	*adj*	croaky, grating, growling, gruff, harsh, husky, rough, throaty
		opposites: clear, smooth
hold	*verb*	1 clasp, cling, detain, embrace, enfold, grasp, grip, possess, take
		2 comprise, contain, retain, support
		3 believe, consider, judge, think
hole	*noun*	aperture, crack, gap, hollow, opening, puncture
hollow	*adj*	concave, empty, unfilled, void
holy	*adj*	devout, divine, pious, religious, sacred, saintly, spiritual, virtuous
		opposites: irreligious, unholy, wicked
honest	*adj*	decent, genuine, open, reliable, sincere, straight, true, trustworthy, truthful, upright
		opposites: deceitful, dishonest, insincere
honourable	*adj*	fair, honest, just, moral, noble, respectable, sincere, straight, true, trustworthy, upright, virtuous
		opposites: dishonest, dishonourable, immoral, insincere
hope	*noun*	ambition, belief, confidence, desire, dream, faith, longing, promise, prospect
		opposites: despair, despondency
	verb	desire, expect, long for, rely on, trust, wish
		opposites: despair, give up
hopeless	*adj*	helpless, incompetent, incurable, unattainable, useless, worthless
		opposites: curable, hopeful, promising

horrible	*adj*	appalling, awful, dreadful, ghastly, grim, grisly, gruesome, hideous, nasty, repulsive, terrible, unpleasant
		opposites: agreeable, pleasant
horrify	*verb*	disgust, frighten, petrify, scare, shock, startle, terrify
		opposites: delight, please
hospitable	*adj*	friendly, generous, kind, sociable, welcoming
		opposites: inhospitable, unkind
hostile	*adj*	aggressive, opposed, unfriendly, unkind, unsympathetic, warlike
		opposites: friendly, peaceable, sympathetic
hot	*adj*	1 boiling, burning, fiery, flaming, heated, roasting, scalding
		opposites: chilly, cold, freezing
		2 excited, fevered, hot-headed, inflamed, passionate
		opposites: bored, indifferent, unexcited
house	*noun*	abode, dwelling, habitation, home, household, lodgings
huddle	*verb*	cluster, congregate, crowd together, gather, press, snuggle, throng
		opposites: disperse, spread out
hug	*verb*	clasp, cling to, cuddle, embrace, hold, squeeze
huge	*adj*	colossal, gigantic, great, immense, large, massive, tremendous, vast
		opposites: small, tiny
humble	*adj*	1 meek, obedient, obsequious, servile, submissive
		opposites: assertive, proud, vain
		2 low, lowly, modest, poor, simple, undistinguished
		opposites: great, important, worthy
humorous	*adj*	amusing, comical, entertaining, funny, merry, witty
		opposites: humourless, serious, solemn, unfunny

hunch	*noun*	feeling, guess, idea, inkling, suspicion
hungry	*adj*	famished, peckish, ravenous, starved, starving
		opposites: full, satisfied
hunt	*verb*	chase, investigate, look for, pursue, rummage, search, seek, stalk, track, trail
hurry	*verb*	accelerate, hasten, look lively, move quickly, quicken, rush, scurry, speed
		opposites: dally, dawdle, delay, take your time
hurt	*verb*	1 ache, be painful
		2 bruise, damage, injure, maim, sting, torture, upset, wound
hypocritical	*adj*	false, hollow, insincere, phoney, two-faced
		opposites: genuine, sincere, true

I

icy	*adj*	1 arctic, bitter, chilly, cold, freezing, frosty, ice-cold
		opposites: warm, hot
		2 aloof, cold, distant, formal, frigid, hostile, reserved, stiff, unfriendly
		opposites: friendly, sociable
idea	*noun*	belief, concept, design, estimate, form, guess, impression, interpretation, notion, opinion, plan, sense, theory, viewpoint
		opposites: actuality, fact
ideal	*noun*	example, model, pattern, perfection, standard
	adj	complete, perfect
identical	*adj*	alike, equal, equivalent, like, matching, same, twin
		opposites: different, unlike
identify	*verb*	classify, detect, distinguish, know, label, name, pick out, pinpoint, place, recognise, specify
idiotic	*adj*	crazy, daft, foolish, insane, moronic, senseless, stupid
		opposites: intelligent, sane, sensible
idle	*adj*	1 jobless, unemployed
		2 good-for-nothing, lazy, shiftless, slothful
		opposites: busy, hard-working
ignorant	*adj*	clueless, illiterate, insensitive, stupid, uneducated, uninformed, untaught, untrained
		opposites: knowledgeable, learned, wise
ignore	*verb*	disregard, neglect, omit, overlook, pass over, reject, take no notice of
		opposites: note, pay attention to
ill	*adj*	not well, poorly, sick, unhealthy, unwell
		opposites: blooming, healthy, well
ill at ease	*adj*	awkward, disturbed, embarrassed, nervous, uncomfortable, uneasy
		opposites: at ease, comfortable, confident

illegal	*adj*	against the law, banned, criminal, forbidden, outlawed, prohibited, unlawful, wrongful
		opposites: legal, right
illness	*noun*	ailment, complaint, disease, ill-health, sickness
		opposites: health, well-being
illogical	*adj*	absurd, irrational, meaningless, senseless, unreasonable, unsound
		opposites: logical, sensible
illustration	*noun*	1 drawing, figure, picture, representation, sketch
		2 example, explanation, instance, specimen
imaginary	*adj*	fanciful, fictitious, hypothetical, imagined, invented, made up, non-existent, unreal
		opposites: actual, real
imitate	*verb*	copy, duplicate, echo, emulate, impersonate, mimic, mirror, mock, reproduce
immature	*adj*	1 babyish, childish, puerile
		opposites: grown-up, sensible
		2 green, raw, undeveloped, unripe
		opposites: fully-grown, ripe
immediately	*adv*	at once, instantly, now, right away, straight off, without delay
		opposites: eventually, later, never
immense	*adj*	enormous, gigantic, huge, large, massive, vast
		opposites: minute, tiny
immodest	*adj*	bold, coarse, immoral, improper, impure, indecent, obscene, shameless
		opposites: chaste, modest, pure
immortal	*adj*	enduring, eternal, everlasting, indestructible, lasting, timeless, underlying
		opposites: mortal, short-lived

impartial	*adj*	equal, even-handed, fair, just, neutral, objective, unprejudiced
		opposites: prejudiced, unfair
impatient	*adj*	abrupt, curt, hasty, impetuous, quick-tempered, restless
		opposites: good-tempered, patient
imperfect	*adj*	broken, damaged, defective, faulty, flawed, incomplete, unfinished
		opposites: perfect, undamaged, whole
impertinent	*adj*	cheeky, discourteous, disrespectful, forward, fresh, ill-mannered, insolent, rude
		opposites: polite, well-mannered
impetuous	*adj*	hasty, impulsive, overeager, rash, unthinking
		opposites: careful, cautious
impolite	*adj*	boorish, disrespectful, ill-bred, ill-mannered, rude
		opposites: polite, well-bred
important	*adj*	essential, influential, meaningful, noteworthy, outstanding, powerful, serious, significant, substantial, valuable
		opposites: insignificant, of no consequence, unimportant
impossible	*adj*	hopeless, ludicrous, outrageous, unreasonable, unthinkable, unworkable
		opposites: achievable, possible
impressive	*adj*	exciting, moving, powerful, striking
		opposites: unexciting, unimpressive
improve	*verb*	correct, develop, enhance, help, increase, mend, recover, rectify, reform
		opposites: decline, diminish, make worse
impudent	*adj*	brazen, cheeky, fresh, impertinent, insolent, rude, shameless
		opposites: polite, well-mannered

impulsive	*adj*	hasty, impetuous, quick, rash, reckless, unpredictable
		opposites: careful, cautious
impure	*adj*	contaminated, corrupt, defiled, dirty, immodest, immoral, indecent, obscene, polluted, tainted, unclean
		opposites: chaste, pure
inaccurate	*adj*	careless, erroneous, faulty, imprecise, incorrect, inexact, mistaken, unreliable, wild, wrong
		opposites: accurate, exact
inadequate	*adj*	1 faulty, imperfect, insufficient, not enough, scanty, sparse
		opposites: adequate, enough, full
		2 incompetent, inefficient
		opposites: competent, efficient
inappropriate	*adj*	ill-suited, improper, out of place, unfit, unfitting, unsuitable
		opposites: appropriate, fitting
incessant	*adj*	ceaseless, continual, continuous, never-ending, non-stop, unceasing
		opposites: sporadic, intermittent
incident	*noun*	adventure, disturbance, episode, event, happening, occurrence, scene
include	*verb*	allow for, encompass, incorporate, involve, rope in, take in
		opposites: exclude, ignore, leave out, reject
incompetent	*adj*	bungling, ineffective, inept, stupid, unfit, unskilled, useless
		opposites: clever, competent, skilled
inconsistent	*adj*	changeable, contradictory, fickle, unpredictable
		opposites: consistent, predictable
inconvenient	*adj*	annoying, awkward, embarrassing, unsuitable, untimely
		opposites: convenient, handy, helpful

incorrect	*adj*	false, faulty, flawed, mistaken, untrue, wrong
		opposites: correct, right, true
increase	*verb*	add to, build up, develop, enlarge, expand, grow, heighten, inflate, multiply, strengthen
		opposites: contract, decrease, weaken
incredible	*adj*	amazing, astonishing, far-fetched, improbable, preposterous, unbelievable
		opposites: believable, probable
indeed	*adv*	actually, certainly, positively, really, strictly, truly, undoubtedly
independent	*adj*	free, self-reliant, self-sufficient, separate, unconnected
		opposites: clinging, dependent
indicate	*verb*	display, express, imply, point out, point to, record, show, signal, suggest
		opposites: conceal, hide
indirect	*adj*	crooked, devious, meandering, rambling, roundabout, tortuous, winding
		opposites: direct, straight
indispensable	*adj*	crucial, essential, imperative, key, necessary, needed, vital
		opposites: not essential, unnecessary
indistinct	*adj*	blurred, confused, faint, hazy, misty, obscure, shadowy, unclear, vague
		opposites: clear, distinct
industrious	*adj*	busy, conscientious, energetic, hard-working, purposeful, tireless
		opposites: lazy, indolent
ineffective	*adj*	feeble, fruitless, inadequate, incompetent, inefficient, useless, weak, worthless
		opposites: effective, strong, useful

inevitable	*adj*	automatic, certain, inescapable, necessary, sure, unavoidable
		opposites: avoidable, uncertain
inferior	*adj*	bad, lesser, lower, poor, poorer, second-class, second-rate, substandard, unsatisfactory, worse
		opposites: better, high-class, superior, top class
infinite	*adj*	boundless, eternal, everlasting, never-ending, total
		opposite: finite
inflame	*verb*	anger, arouse, enrage, excite, increase, infuriate, madden, provoke
		opposites: calm down, cool, mollify
influence	*noun*	control, mastery, power, prestige, strength, sway, teaching, training
	verb	affect, change, control, guide, persuade
inform	*verb*	advise, enlighten, instruct, notify, teach, tell
		opposites: keep in the dark, mislead
infrequent	*adj*	occasional, rare, uncommon, unusual
		opposites: frequent, usual
inhabit	*verb*	dwell, live, occupy, reside, settle in, stay
injure	*verb*	cripple, damage, disfigure, harm, hurt, ill-treat, maim, wound
		opposites: heal, help
innocent	*adj*	chaste, faultless, harmless, open, pure, spotless, trustful, trusting, unsuspicious
		opposites: bad, evil, guilty, suspicious
inquire	*verb*	ask, enquire, explore, investigate, look into, question, search
inquisitive	*adj*	curious, nosy, prying, questioning, snooping
		opposites: incurious, unquestioning

insane	*adj*	demented, deranged, lunatic, mad, unbalanced, unhinged
		opposites: sane, sensible, well-balanced
insert	*verb*	introduce, let in, place, put in, stick in
		opposites: extract, pull out, take out
insignificant	*adj*	inconsequential, insubstantial, meaningless, minor, tiny, unimportant
		opposites: important, significant
inspect	*verb*	examine, look over, scan, scrutinise, search, study
inspire	*verb*	arouse, encourage, excite, motivate, spark off, stimulate
		opposites: deflate, depress, discourage
instant	*noun*	flash, jiffy, minute, moment, second, twinkling
		opposites: age, long time
	adj	fast, immediate, instantaneous, on-the-spot, quick, rapid, urgent
		opposites: delayed, slow
instruct	*verb*	advise, coach, direct, discipline, drill, educate, guide, inform, notify, order, teach, tell, train, tutor
		opposites: follow, learn, obey
insult	*verb*	abuse, call names, offend, revile, slander, snub
		opposites: compliment, praise
intelligent	*adj*	brainy, bright, clever, quick, quick-witted, sharp, smart, well-informed
		opposites: foolish, slow, unintelligent
intention	*noun*	aim, design, goal, idea, meaning, objective, plan, purpose, target
intentional	*adj*	deliberate, intended, meant, planned, prearranged
		opposites: accidental, by chance, unplanned
interest	*noun*	1 attention, business, care, concern, matter, preoccupation, study

		opposites: boredom, irrelevance

2 benefit, gain, portion, profit, stake
opposite: loss

interesting	*adj*	1 amusing, appealing, attractive, entertaining, gripping, stimulating, thought-provoking

opposites: boring, dull, uninteresting

2 curious, intriguing, unusual
opposites: humdrum, ordinary

interior	*adj*	central, inland, inner, inside, internal, inward

opposites: exterior, outside, outward

internal	*adj*	inner, inside, interior, private

opposites: external, outside

interrupt	*verb*	1 barge in, butt in, interfere, interject, intrude

opposite: leave alone

2 break off, cut off, disconnect, discontinue, divide, separate, stop
opposites: connect, join up

introduce	*verb*	begin, bring in, initiate, inject, launch, lead into, offer, present, put forward

opposites: keep back, withdraw

invade	*verb*	attack, burst in, enter, occupy, overrun, raid, seize

opposites: retreat, withdraw

invent	*verb*	conceive, create, design, devise, dream up, imagine, make up, think up

investigate	*verb*	consider, examine, explore, inspect, scrutinise, search, study

invite	*verb*	ask, ask for, beg, call, draw, encourage, request, seek, summon

opposites: force, order

involve	*verb*	comprise, concern, draw in, engage, hold, include, require, take in
		opposites: exclude, keep out
irregular	*adj*	abnormal, crooked, erratic, haphazard, jagged, odd, peculiar, ragged, wavering
		opposites: even, regular, smooth
irritable	*adj*	bad-tempered, crusty, prickly, short-tempered, touchy
		opposites: cheerful, good-humoured
irritate	*verb*	anger, annoy, bother, infuriate, offend, pester
		opposites: gratify, please

jab   *verb*   elbow, nudge, poke, prod, push, shove, thrust

jaded   *adj*   exhausted, fatigued, tired
opposites: fresh, lively, full of spirits

jagged   *adj*   irregular, notched, pointed, ragged, saw-edged, serrated, spiked, uneven
opposites: smooth, straight-edged

jam   *verb*   cram, crowd, crush, pack, press, ram, squash, squeeze, stick, thrust
opposites: free, release

jaunty   *adj*   carefree, cheeky, high-spirited, lively, perky, sprightly
opposites: anxious, depressed, dull

jealous   *adj*   covetous, envious, green-eyed, possessive, resentful, wary
opposites: content, tolerant, trusting

jeer   *verb*   deride, heckle, mock, ridicule, scoff at, sneer at, taunt
opposites: applaud, cheer, encourage

jewel   *noun*   1 gem, gemstone, pearl, precious stone
2 prize, rarity, treasure

jilt   *verb*   abandon, desert, ditch, drop, reject, spurn
opposites: accept, cling to, marry

jittery   *adj*   anxious, edgy, flustered, jumpy, nervous, quivering, uneasy
opposites: calm, cool, self-possessed

job   *noun*   business, career, employment, livelihood, occupation, profession, situation, vocation

join   *verb*   1 accompany, link up with, merge with, team up with
opposites: break off from, leave

2 add, append, combine, couple, fasten, merge, tie
opposites: uncouple, untie

3 enlist, enter, sign up
opposite: resign from

jolly   *adj*   cheerful, cheery, funny, happy, jovial, merry, playful
opposites: sad, serious

jolt   *verb*   1   bump, disturb, jar, jerk, knock, push, shake, shove

2   shock, startle, surprise

journey   *noun*   expedition, outing, pilgrimage, ramble, safari, tour, trip, voyage

joy   *noun*   bliss, delight, ecstasy, gaiety, gladness, glee, happiness, pleasure
opposites: misery, sadness, unhappiness

judge   *verb*   adjudicate, assess, consider, decide, estimate, examine, try

jumbled   *adj*   confused, disordered, disorganised, mixed-up, muddled, tangled, untidy
opposites: neat, organised, tidy

jump   *verb*   1   bounce, dance, hop, leap, prance, skip, spring, vault

2   increase, mount, rise
opposites: decline, drop

just   *adj*   1   even-handed, fair, fair-minded, impartial, reasonable, true, unbiased
opposites: biased, unfair, unjust

2   due, fitting, lawful, legitimate
opposites: illegitimate, unlawful

justifiable   *adj*   allowable, excusable, forgivable, lawful, pardonable, reasonable, right, understandable
opposites: illicit, unjustifiable

juvenile   *noun*   adolescent, boy, girl, minor, young person, youth
opposites: adult, grown-up

K

keen	*adj*	eager, enthusiastic, industrious, sharp, zealous
		opposites: apathetic, laid back, unenthusiastic

keep	*verb*	1 hang on to, hold, hold on to, maintain, possess, retain, store
		opposites: let go, give up, release
		2 care for, feed, guard, look after, nourish, protect, shelter, support, watch over
		opposites: ignore, neglect

kill	*verb*	assassinate, do away with, execute, murder, put to death, slaughter
		opposites: preserve, protect, spare

kind	*noun*	brand, breed, category, family, type, variety
	adj	considerate, generous, kindly, neighbourly, thoughtful, understanding
		opposites: inconsiderate, selfish, unkind

knack	*noun*	ability, aptitude, flair, genius, gift, skill, talent
knock	*verb*	hit, punch, rap, slap, smack, strike, thump
know	*verb*	be aware of, comprehend, realise, recognise, understand
		opposites: be ignorant of, fail to understand

knowledge	*noun*	awareness, education, information, instruction, intelligence, learning, understanding
		opposites: ignorance, stupidity

knowledgeable	*adj*	aware, educated, experienced, well-informed
		opposites: clueless, ignorant, stupid

L

label	*noun*	badge, description, mark, marker, name, stamp, sticker, tag, ticket, trademark
	verb	clarify, define, describe, name
labour	*noun*	1 drudgery, effort, exertion, industry, toil, work
		opposites: comfort, ease, leisure
		2 birth, childbirth, delivery
	verb	strive, struggle, toil, work
lack	*noun*	absence, emptiness, need, scarcity, shortage, want
		opposites: abundance, plenty
	verb	be without, miss, need, not have, require, want
		opposite: have
lame	*verb*	cripple, damage, injure, maim
	adj	1 crippled, disabled, handicapped, injured, limping
		opposites: uninjured, whole
		2 feeble, poor, unconvincing, unsatisfactory, weak
		opposites: acceptable, adequate, satisfactory
land	*noun*	1 country, district, nation, region, territory
		2 countryside, estate, grounds, property
		3 earth, ground, soil
	verb	alight, arrive, disembark, dock, go ashore, touch down
		opposites: embark, board, go aboard, take off
large	*adj*	big, broad, bulky, great, huge, immense, long, massive, spacious, vast, wide
		opposites: little, minute, small, tiny
last	*noun*	conclusion, end, finish
		opposites: first, initial, opening
	verb	carry on, continue, hold on, hold out, keep on, remain, stay, survive
		opposites: disappear, end, fade away, stop

	adj	1 concluding, final
		opposites: beginning, first
		2 latest, most recent
		opposites: first, original
	adv	after, finally
		opposites: first, firstly, initially

lasting   *adj*   continuing, enduring, lifelong, long-term, unceasing, unending

opposites: fleeting, short-lived, temporary

late   *adj*   1 behind, belated, delayed, last-minute, overdue, unpunctual

opposites: early, punctual

2 dead, deceased

laugh   *verb*   chortle, chuckle, giggle, guffaw, snigger, titter

opposites: cry, sob, weep

laugh at   *verb*   make fun of, mock, ridicule, scoff at, taunt

opposites: praise, take seriously

laughter   *noun*   amusement, giggling, hilarity, laughing, merriment, mirth

opposites: crying, sadness

law   *noun*   command, decree, order, regulation, rule, statute

lawful   *adj*   allowable, legal, permissible, proper, rightful

opposites: illegal, unlawful

layer   *noun*   coat, coating, covering, deposit, film, sheet, thickness

lazy   *adj*   idle, inactive, lackadaisical, slothful, slow-moving, work-shy

opposites: active, busy, diligent, energetic

lead	*noun*	1	first place, leadership, principal, title role
		2	clue, suggestion
	verb	1	go in front of, guide, head
			opposites: come after, follow
		2	command, control, govern
			opposites: obey, serve

leader   *noun*   captain, chief, commander, guide, manager, ruler
opposites: follower, supporter

leaflet   *noun*   booklet, brochure, circular, flyer, handout

leak   *noun*   discharge, escape, drip
             verb   drip, escape, flow out, ooze, trickle out

lean   *verb*   bend, incline, slant, slope
opposite: straighten up

           adj   1   bony, lank, scrawny, skinny, slim, thin, wiry
                     opposites: fat, well-fleshed

                      2   poor, scanty, sparse
                     opposites: full, rich

leap   *noun*   bound, hop, jump, skip, spring

learn   *verb*   discover, find out, hear, grasp, master, memorise, pick up, understand

learning   *noun*   education, knowledge, scholarship, study, wisdom

leave   *verb*   abandon, desert, go away, take off, withdraw
opposites: arrive, come

legal   *adj*   allowable, allowed, lawful, legitimate, permissible
opposites: illegal, not allowed, unlawful

legendary   *adj*   fabulous, famous, fictional, renowned, well-known

legitimate   *adj*   genuine, justifiable, lawful, rightful, true
opposites: illegitimate, unlawful

leisure   *noun*   ease, freedom, recreation, relaxation, rest *opposites:* toil, work

lessen	*verb*	contract, curtail, decrease, diminish, dwindle, reduce, shrink, weaken

opposites: expand, extend, increase

let   *verb*   agree to, allow, give permission, permit

opposites: forbid, prevent

level   *adj*   1 balanced, equal, even

opposite: uneven

2 flat, horizontal, smooth

opposites: inclined, irregular, up and down

lie   *verb*   1 falsify, fib, misrepresent, tell a lie

opposite: tell the truth

2 laze, loll, lounge, recline, rest, stretch out

lift   *verb*   pick up, raise, take up, uplift

opposites: drop, let fall, put down

light   *noun*   blaze, bulb, daylight, flame, flare, gleam, glint, glow, sparkle, sunshine

opposites: dark, darkness, shade

adj   delicate, flimsy, not heavy, unsubstantial

opposites: heavy, weighty

verb   ignite, set fire to

like   *verb*   delight in, enjoy, fancy, love, relish

opposites: detest, dislike

likeable   *adj*   agreeable, attractive, friendly, lovable, nice, pleasant

opposites: disagreeable, unattractive, unlikeable

limit   *noun*   border, boundary, brink, edge, end, periphery, terminus, verge

linger   *verb*   dawdle, idle, loiter, remain, stay, wait

opposites: leave, rush off

link   *verb*   attach, bracket, connect, couple, fasten, join, unite
                             opposites: disconnect, separate

list   *noun*   catalogue, index, inventory, register, roll, table

litter   *noun*   clutter, mess, refuse, rubbish, waste

little   *adj*   paltry, petty, short, small, tiny, undeveloped
                             opposites: big, large, long

live   *verb*   breathe, draw breath, exist, survive
                             opposite: die

                    adj   alive, energetic, lively, living, vigorous
                             opposites: dead, lifeless

lively   *adj*   active, alert, bright, bustling, cheerful, energetic,
                             frisky, sparkling, vivacious
                             opposites: dull, lifeless

lock   *verb*   bolt, fasten, secure, shut
                             opposites: unfasten, unlock

lonely   *adj*   alone, forsaken, friendless, lonesome, solitary

long   *adj*   elongated, expanded, extended, lengthy, spread out,
                             stretched
                             opposites: brief, fleeting, short

look   *verb*   examine, gaze, inspect, observe, scan, see, stare,
                             view, watch

loosen   *verb*   detach, let go, release, set free, slacken, undo,
                             unfasten, untie
                             opposite: tighten

lose   *verb*   1 drop, mislay, misplace
                                opposites: find, recover

                             2 be defeated, come to grief, fail, suffer defeat
                                opposites: succeed, win

loud   *adj*   1 blaring, booming, deafening, piercing, thundering
                                opposites: low, quiet, soft

2 brash, coarse, crude, loud-mouthed, vulgar

opposite: refined

love	*verb*	adore, desire, enjoy, idolise, like, treasure, worship
		opposites: detest, hate, loathe
lovely	*adj*	adorable, attractive, beautiful, pleasing, pretty
		opposites: hideous, unattractive, ugly
loyal	*adj*	dependable, devoted, faithful, patriotic, sincere, trustworthy
		opposites: disloyal, traitorous
luck	*noun*	break, chance, fate, good fortune, success
		opposite: misfortune
lucky	*adj*	charmed, favoured, fortunate, successful
		opposite: unlucky
lukewarm	*adj*	apathetic, cool, half-hearted, indifferent, unenthusiastic, uninterested
		opposites: enthusiastic, passionate
luscious	*adj*	appetising, delicious, juicy, mouth-watering, scrumptious, succulent, tasty
luxury	*noun*	affluence, comfort, extravagance, opulence, richness, well-being
		opposites: need, poverty, want

M

mad	*adj*	1 crazy, foolish, insane, irrational, unstable *opposites:* sensible, sane
		2 angry, enraged, fuming, infuriated, raging *opposites:* friendly, peaceable
magic	*noun*	hocus pocus, illusion, sorcery, trickery, witchcraft, wizardry
	adj	amazing, magical, marvellous, miraculous, spellbinding, wonderful *opposites:* humdrum, ordinary
magnificent	*adj*	brilliant, excellent, glorious, grand, impressive, noble, splendid *opposites:* humble, modest, plain, simple
magnify	*verb*	build up, enhance, expand, increase, exaggerate, intensify, overrate *opposites:* belittle, play down
maim	*verb*	cripple, damage, injure, lame, mutilate, wound
main	*adj*	central, chief, first, foremost, primary, principal, supreme, vital *opposites:* minor, unimportant
maintain	*verb*	1 care for, conserve, defend, keep up, look after, preserve, support, take care of *opposites:* abandon, desert, neglect
		2 claim, declare, hold, profess, state, uphold *opposites:* deny, oppose
majestic	*adj*	dignified, grand, noble, regal, splendid, superb *opposites:* unimportant, unimpressive
major	*adj*	chief, crucial, greater, important, leading, main, outstanding, senior, uppermost *opposites:* least, minor
make	*verb*	1 assemble, bring about, build, create, fashion, form, produce, put together, shape

		opposites: break up, demolish, dismantle, undo
		2 compel, force, induce, oblige, pressurise
		opposites: invite, persuade
man	*noun*	adult, gentleman, male
		opposites: female, woman
manage	*verb*	1 achieve, accomplish, bring about, do, cope with, succeed in
		opposites: fail, mismanage
		2 control, direct, guide, influence, operate, run, use
		opposites: be guided, serve
manageable	*adj*	controllable, docile, easygoing, submissive
		opposites: awkward, unmanageable
mankind	*noun*	human race, humanity, man
manner	*noun*	1 appearance, behaviour, character, conduct, demeanour
		2 kind, method, nature, style, type, way
manners	*noun*	behaviour, conduct, politeness, refinement, social graces
		opposites: discourtesy, impoliteness, vulgarity
manufacture	*verb*	build, construct, devise, make, mass-produce, turn out
many	*adj*	countless, frequent, innumerable, numerous, umpteen, various
		opposites: few, infrequent
march	*verb*	pace, parade, stride, strut, tramp, trek, walk briskly
marginal	*adj*	borderline, doubtful, insignificant, minor, slight, small
		opposites: central, great, important
mark	*verb*	nick, scar, scratch, smudge, stain, streak
		opposites: clean, clear, renovate
	noun	1 blemish, blot, dent, scar, scratch, smudge, streak, trace
		2 badge, emblem, feature, seal, sign, symbol

maroon	*verb*	abandon, isolate, leave in danger, put ashore
		opposite: rescue
marsh	*noun*	bog, marshland, morass, quagmire, swamp, wetland
marvellous	*adj*	amazing, astonishing, excellent, extraordinary, fantastic, glorious, incredible, magnificent, miraculous, sensational, superb, wonderful
		opposites: ordinary, unexciting
mass	*noun*	1 bulk, heap, lump, piece, pile, quantity, size
		2 collection, crowd, group, horde, lot, majority, mob, number, sum, whole
		opposites: individual, item
massacre	*noun*	blood bath, carnage, killing, mass murder, slaughter
massive	*adj*	enormous, gigantic, huge, immense, vast, weighty
		opposites: slight, small
master	*verb*	1 acquire, get the hang of, grasp, learn
		2 control, dominate, manage, rule, subdue, suppress, vanquish
		opposites: be subservient to, follow, serve
mastery	*noun*	ability, expertise, grasp, prowess, skill, understanding
		opposites: clumsiness, unfamiliarity
match	*verb*	1 combine, join, link, pair, unite
		opposites: detach, separate
		2 compare, equal
		opposites: oppose, rival
material	*noun*	1 cloth, fabric, stuff, textile
		2 data, facts, information, matter
matter	*verb*	count, make a difference, mean something, signify
		opposites: be irrelevant, make no difference
	noun	business, concern, difficulty, occurrence, problem, significance, topic, transaction, trouble, worry

mature	*adj*	adult, complete, full-grown, grown-up, ready, ripe
		opposites: juvenile, immature, unready
maximum	*adj*	biggest, greatest, highest, largest, most, supreme
		opposites: least, minimum
mean	*verb*	convey, denote, indicate, intend, plan, promise, say, signify, suggest
	adj	1 miserly, penny-pinching, selfish, tight-fisted, ungenerous
		opposites: generous, giving, open-handed
		2 contemptible, disgraceful, low, miserable, unpleasant, vicious, vile
		opposites: honourable, noble
		3 average, halfway, median, middle, standard
		opposite: extreme
meaning	*noun*	drift, intention, message, plan, point, purpose, sense
		opposite: nonsense
meaningless	*adj*	absurd, futile, insignificant, nonsensical, pointless, useless, worthless
		opposites: meaningful, significant, valuable
means	*noun*	1 funds, income, money, riches, wealth
		opposites: lack of funds, poverty
		2 ability, method, technique, way
		opposite: inability
measure	*verb*	calculate, estimate, evaluate, judge, size up, weigh up
mediocre	*adj*	average, insignificant, middling, ordinary, passable, second-rate
		opposites: excellent, exceptional, superior
meek	*adj*	humble, slavish, submissive, weak
		opposites: self-assured, strong

meet	*verb*	1 bump into, come across, contact, encounter, find, join, run across, run into
		opposites: avoid, miss
		2 answer, fulfil, match, measure up to
		opposite: fail
melancholy	*adj*	depressed, down-in-the-dumps, gloomy, sad, unhappy
		opposites: cheerful, happy, joyful
melt	*verb*	dissolve, liquefy, soften, thaw, unfreeze
		opposites: freeze, harden, solidify
memorise	*verb*	commit to memory, learn, learn by heart, swot up on
		opposites: forget, put aside
menace	*noun*	1 annoyance, nuisance, pest, troublemaker
		2 danger, hazard, peril, terror, threat, warning
mend	*verb*	correct, cure, fix, improve, patch, rectify, repair
		opposites: break, damage, destroy
mention	*verb*	bring up, disclose, make known, name, refer to, reveal, state, tell
		opposites: conceal, keep quiet about
merciless	*adj*	cruel, heartless, pitiless, relentless, ruthless, unforgiving
		opposites: forgiving, merciful
mercy	*noun*	compassion, forgiveness, kindness, pity, relief
		opposites: cruelty, revenge
merge	*verb*	blend, combine, fuse, intermix, join, mix, unite
		opposites: disconnect, separate
merit	*noun*	credit, excellence, quality, virtue, worth
		opposites: fault, worthlessness
	verb	deserve, earn, win
mess	*noun*	clutter, disorder, jumble, litter, muddle, shambles
		opposites: order, tidiness

message	*noun*	communication, idea, letter, meaning, note, notice, word
method	*noun*	approach, manner, organisation, pattern, plan, structure, style, system, way
		opposites: disorder, lack of structure
methodical	*adj*	businesslike, efficient, neat, orderly, organised, systematic
		opposites: confused, disorganised, unmethodical
middle	*adj*	central, halfway, inner, inside, mid, mid-point
		opposites: exterior, outside
	noun	centre, halfway point, heart, inside, mid-point
		opposites: beginning, border, edge, end, extreme
mild	*adj*	gentle, mellow, moderate, pleasant, smooth, tender
		opposites: fierce, harsh, stormy
mimic	*verb*	ape, imitate, impersonate, look like, resemble
mind	*noun*	brains, head, imagination, intellect, memory, reason, sense, thoughts, wits
mine	*verb*	dig for, excavate, extract, tunnel, unearth
		opposite: bury
mingle	*verb*	blend, combine, intermix, join, merge, mix, unite
		opposites: separate, tease apart
minimum	*adj*	least, lowest, slightest, smallest
		opposites: maximum, most
minor	*adj*	insignificant, lesser, petty, secondary, trivial, unimportant
		opposites: important, major, senior
minute	*adj*	infinitesimal, little, paltry, slight, small, tiny, unimportant
		opposites: gigantic, huge, immense

miraculous	*adj*	amazing, astonishing, inexplicable, magical, marvellous, supernatural, wonderful
		opposites: natural, ordinary, unsurprising
mirth	*noun*	amusement, fun, jollity, laughter, pleasure
		opposites: gloom, melancholy
mischief	*noun*	harm, hurt, injury, trouble
misconduct	*noun*	bad behaviour, immorality, rudeness, wrongdoing
		opposites: good behaviour, virtue
miserable	*adj*	1 dejected, gloomy, heartbroken, mournful, sad, sorrowful
		opposites: cheery, happy
		2 paltry, pathetic, poor, vile, worthless
		opposites: generous, noble
misfortune	*noun*	bad luck, disaster, grief, hardship, harm, trouble
		opposites: good luck, success
mislead	*verb*	deceive, fool, misinform, take in
		opposites: inform, tell the truth
miss	*verb*	1 avoid, bypass, evade, go past, omit, overlook, pass over, sidestep
		opposites: confront, hit, strike
		2 grieve for, lament, long for, mourn, regret, want, yearn for
		opposites: enjoy, have
mission	*noun*	aim, business, duty, errand, goal, object, purpose, task, work
mist	*noun*	cloud, dew, fog, haze, spray, vapour
mistake	*noun*	blunder, error, fault, misjudgement, oversight, slip, slip-up
mix	*verb*	blend, combine, cross, join, merge, unite
		opposites: segregate, separate

moan	*verb*	complain, grumble, sigh, wail, whimper
		opposite: rejoice
mock	*verb*	jeer at, laugh at, make fun of, ridicule, taunt, tease
		opposites: flatter, praise
model	*noun*	example, ideal, image, pattern, representation, type, yardstick
	adj	exemplary, first-class, ideal, perfect
		opposites: imperfect, poor, second-rate
moderate	*adj*	average, mediocre, middling, mild, ordinary
		opposites: exceptional, special, outstanding
modern	*adj*	advanced, fashionable, latest, new, present-day, recent, up-to-date
		opposites: antiquated, old, out-of-date
modest	*adj*	bashful, humble, quiet, shy, unassuming
		opposites: conceited, vain
moist	*adj*	damp, humid, muggy, soggy, wet
		opposites: arid, dry
moment	*noun*	instant, jiffy, minute, split second, twinkling
monster	*noun*	demon, devil, fiend, freak, giant, ogre
	adj	colossal, enormous, gigantic, monstrous, tremendous
		opposites: small, tiny
moral	*adj*	good, honest, honourable, noble, pure, straight, virtuous
		opposites: bad, immoral
morsel	*noun*	bit, fragment, grain, mouthful, piece, scrap
motion	*noun*	action, flow, gesture, movement, nod, sign, signal, wave
		opposites: inaction, inactivity
motionless	*adj*	at rest, fixed, frozen, stationary, still, unmoving
		opposites: active, moving

mount   *verb*   ascend, climb, get on, get up
                           opposites: descend, get down, go down

move   *verb*   1 advance, get going, go, proceed, walk
                              opposites: stay still, stop

                           2 carry, propel, transfer
                              opposites: leave alone, leave behind

                           3 affect, make sad, touch
                              opposites: leave unmoved, leave untouched

muddle   *noun*   chaos, clutter, disorder, disorganisation, jumble,
                           mess, tangle
                           opposites: order, organisation

murder   *noun*   assassination, homicide, killing, manslaughter,
                           massacre, slaughter, slaying

                   verb   assassinate, do in, kill, slay
                           opposites: preserve, protect, spare

musty   *adj*   airless, dark, fusty, mouldy, smelly, stale
                           opposites: airy, fresh, sweet-smelling

mutter   *verb*   mumble, murmur, speak under the breath
                           opposites: shout, speak up

mysterious   *adj*   baffling, curious, hidden, inexplicable, puzzling,
                           secret, strange, weird
                           opposites: comprehensible, frank, open,
                           straightforward

mystery   *noun*   conundrum, puzzle, question, riddle, secret
                           opposites: answer, solution

myth   *noun*   fable, fairy tale, fiction, legend, superstition
                           opposites: fact, reality

N

nag	*verb*	annoy, harass, pester, scold, torment
naked	*adj*	bare, nude, unclothed
		opposites: clothed, covered
name	*noun*	designation, label, nickname, term, title
narrow	*adj*	1 cramped, slender, slim, tapering, thin, tight
		opposites: broad, open, wide
		2 bigoted, narrow-minded, prejudiced
		opposites: generous, unprejudiced, tolerant
nasty	*adj*	bad, disgusting, filthy, horrible, loathsome, odious, spiteful, unpleasant, vile
		opposites: decent, good, pleasant
natural	*adj*	genuine, normal, ordinary, plain, real, simple
		opposites: abnormal, artificial, unnatural
nature	*noun*	1 creation, environment, universe, world
		2 category, description, essence, kind, type, variety
naughty	*adj*	bad, disobedient, mischievous, wayward
		opposites: good, polite, well-behaved
nearly	*adv*	all but, almost, approximately, not quite, practically, roughly
		opposites: entirely, totally
neat	*adj*	1 shipshape, smart, spick-and-span, tidy
		opposites: disordered, untidy
		2 clever, efficient, elegant, skilful, systematic
		opposites: clumsy, messy
necessary	*adj*	essential, indispensable, needed, required, vital
		opposites: inessential, unimportant, unnecessary
need	*verb*	demand, require, want
	noun	distress, lack, necessity, poverty, shortage
		opposites: comfort, well-being

neglect	*verb*	ignore, leave alone, omit, overlook, slight, spurn
		opposites: care for, look after, take care of
negotiate	*verb*	arrange, bargain, discuss, settle
neighbourhood	*noun*	community, district, locality, surroundings, vicinity
nervous	*adj*	anxious, excitable, flustered, jumpy, shaky, tense, uneasy, worried
		opposites: confident, cool, relaxed
neutral	*adj*	1 colourless, dull, nondescript
		opposites: striking, vivid
		2 even-handed, impartial, unbiased
		opposites: biased, prejudiced
new	*adj*	1 fresh, latest, modern, recent, unused
		opposites: old, outdated
		2 different, improved, original, unknown, unusual
		opposites: old fashioned, same, usual
nice	*adj*	attractive, charming, courteous, delightful, good, likeable, pleasant, well-mannered
		opposites: nasty, unpleasant
nimble	*adj*	active, agile, brisk, lively, quick, smart, sprightly
		opposites: awkward, clumsy
nip	*verb*	bite, grip, nibble, pinch, squeeze, tweak
noble	*adj*	dignified, distinguished, great, honourable, splendid, upright, virtuous
		opposites: dishonourable, mean, unworthy
noise	*noun*	clamour, din, hubbub, racket, row, uproar
		opposites: quiet, silence
nominate	*verb*	appoint, choose, name, propose, recommend, suggest
nonsense	*noun*	drivel, foolishness, rubbish, silliness, stupidity, twaddle
		opposites: logic, sense

normal	*adj*	common, ordinary, regular, standard, typical, usual
		opposites: abnormal, odd, peculiar, unusual
notable	*adj*	eminent, famous, noteworthy, outstanding, rare, well-known
		opposites: common-or-garden, ordinary, usual
note	*noun*	1 letter, line, memo, message, notice
		2 fame, reputation,
	verb	mark, mention, notice, observe, record, remark
		opposites: omit, overlook
notice	*noun*	announcement, communication, instruction, notification, poster, sign
	verb	detect, heed, note, observe, see, spot
		opposites: disregard, ignore, miss
notify	*verb*	advise, alert, inform, tell, warn
		opposites: keep secret, say nothing
nourish	*verb*	feed, foster, look after, nurse, support, sustain
		opposites: deprive, starve
novice	*noun*	beginner, learner, newcomer, pupil
		opposites: expert, old-hand
nude	*adj*	bare, naked, unclothed, uncovered, undressed
		opposites: clothed, covered, dressed
nuisance	*noun*	annoyance, bore, irritation, pain-in-the-neck, pest, problem, trouble
		opposites: assistance, help
number	*noun*	1 amount, digit, figure, numeral, quantity, sum, total, unit
		2 crowd, many, multitude, several
		opposite: few
numerous	*adj*	abundant, a lot of, lots, many, various
		opposites: few, not many

O

obedient	*adj*	dutiful, law-abiding, respectful, well-trained
		opposites: disobedient, rebellious
obey	*verb*	1 be ruled by, follow, serve, submit to
		opposites: disobey, oppose
		2 carry out, keep, implement, observe
		opposites: ignore
object	*noun*	1 article, item, thing
		2 aim, design, goal, intention, purpose, reason
obnoxious	*adj*	disgusting, foul, hateful, nasty, offensive, sickening
		opposites: agreeable, likeable, pleasant
obscene	*adj*	coarse, dirty, foul, immoral, impure, indecent, offensive, smutty
		opposites: clean, decent, pure
obscure	*adj*	blurred, clouded, confusing, doubtful, hazy, hidden, indistinct, mysterious, shadowy
		opposites: clear, definite, explicit
observant	*adj*	alert, attentive, sharp-eyed, watchful, wide-awake
		opposites: inattentive, unobservant
observe	*verb*	1 keep an eye on, perceive, see, spot, study, survey, watch, witness
		opposites: miss, overlook
		2 abide by, follow, heed, obey, respect
		opposites: break, ignore, violate
obstacle	*noun*	barrier, check, difficulty, drawback, hurdle, obstruction, stumbling-block
		opposites: advantage, help
obstinate	*adj*	headstrong, inflexible, self-willed, stubborn, unyielding
		opposites: adaptable, cooperative, flexible
obstruct	*verb*	hamper, hinder, prevent, restrict, stop, thwart
		opposites: aid, assist, help

obtain	*verb*	acquire, come by, earn, gain, get, secure
		opposites: give back, give up, lose, return
obvious	*adj*	clear, evident, glaring, plain, self-evident, unmistakeable
		opposites: hidden, obscure, unclear
occasional	*adj*	casual, infrequent, irregular, now and then, rare, uncommon
		opposites: frequent, regular
occasionally	*adv*	at times, from time to time, infrequently, now and again, once in a while, periodically, sometimes
		opposites: frequently, often
occupation	*noun*	business, calling, career, craft, employment, job, post, trade, vocation, work
occupy	*verb*	conquer, hold, invade, seize, take over, take possession of
		opposites: give up, surrender
occur	*verb*	come about, crop up, happen, show itself, take place, transpire
occurrence	*noun*	circumstance, episode, event, happening, incident
odd	*adj*	1 not even, single, uneven, unmatched, various
		opposite: even
		2 curious, different, extraordinary, irregular, peculiar, queer, strange, unusual, weird
		opposites: normal, ordinary, usual
odour	*noun*	aroma, bouquet, fragrance, perfume, scent, smell
offence	*noun*	crime, fault, insult, sin, slight, snub, wrong, wrongdoing
offensive	*adj*	annoying, disagreeable, disgusting, insulting, loathsome, nasty, obnoxious, revolting, rude, unpleasant
		opposites: charming, pleasant, pleasing

offer	*verb*	give, hold out, present, provide, show, suggest, volunteer
		opposites: take back, withdraw
officer	*noun*	administrator, agent, executive, functionary, official, public servant, representative
official	*adj*	approved, authorised, certified, proper
		opposites: informal, unofficial
old	*adj*	1 antique, dated, long-standing, original, primitive
		opposites: new, recent, young
		2 crumbling, decrepit, old-fashioned, unwanted, worn-out
		opposites: fresh, useful, youthful
omit	*verb*	drop, exclude, forget, leave out, neglect, overlook, pass over, skip
		opposites: add, attend to, include
ooze	*verb*	discharge, drain, drip, escape, leak, seep, weep
		opposites: gush, pour out
open	*adj*	1 exposed, evident, noticeable, obvious, public, spacious, uncovered, vacant, visible
		opposites: closed, covered, shut
		2 candid, frank, generous, innocent, sincere, unprejudiced
		opposites: dishonest, insincere, secretive
opening	*noun*	1 aperture, chink, crack, gap, hole, rent, rupture, space
		opposites: bar, barrier, cover
		2 beginning, birth, chance, launch, occasion, opportunity, start
		opposites: closing, closure, ending
operate	*verb*	act, handle, manage, perform, run, use, utilise, work

opinion	*noun*	belief, feeling, idea, impression, judgement, notion, point of view, theory, view *opposites:* certainty, fact
opponent	*noun*	adversary, competitor, enemy, rival *opposites:* ally, friend, helper
opportunity	*noun*	chance, opening, time, turn
oppose	*verb*	attack, confront, counter, defy, face, fight, hinder, obstruct, prevent, resist, stand up to, withstand *opposites:* aid, favour, go along with, support
opposite	*adj*	contrary, different, differing, diverse, hostile, opposed, reverse, unlike *opposites:* like, same, similar
opposition	*noun*	clash, competition, hostility, other side, rival *opposites:* ally, cooperation, support, supporter
oppress	*verb*	crush, harass, harry, overpower, torment, tyrannise *opposites:* help, support
optimistic	*adj*	bright, cheerful, confident, hopeful, positive, upbeat *opposites:* crushed, deflated, pessimistic
option	*noun*	alternative, choice, possibility, preference, selection
oral	*adj*	said, spoken, verbal, vocal *opposite:* written
order	*noun*	1 command, directive, law, regulation, rule 2 arrangement, classification, grouping, layout, neatness, organisation, pattern, plan, sequence, series, structure, system *opposites:* disorder, jumble, mess
	verb	1 book, request, reserve 2 command, decree, direct, instruct, manage, require
orderly	*adj*	businesslike, methodical, neat, systematic, tidy, well-organised *opposites:* disorderly, messy, unsystematic

ordinary	*adj*	average, common, everyday, familiar, mediocre, plain, routine, standard, undistinguished, usual
		opposites: extraordinary, special, unusual
organisation	*noun*	1 association, body, company, firm, group, outfit
		2 arrangement, design, formation, method, pattern, plan, structure, system
		opposites: disorganisation, untidiness
origin	*noun*	beginning, beginnings, birth, creation, launch, source, start
		opposites: end, finish
original	*adj*	1 earliest, first, new, primary, primitive
		opposites: latest, recent
		2 creative, fresh, imaginative, inventive, unusual
		opposites: jaded, run-of-the-mill, unoriginal
originate	*verb*	be born, come, emerge, proceed, spring, start
		opposites: end, finish, terminate
ornament	*noun*	decoration, frill, garnish, jewel, trinket
outbreak	*noun*	epidemic, eruption, explosion, flare-up, outburst, upsurge
outdo	*verb*	beat, get the better of, outclass, outfox, outsmart, outwit, overcome, surpass
		opposites: be defeated, succumb
outlet	*noun*	avenue, channel, duct, exit, opening, safety valve, way out
		opposites: inlet, way in
outrageous	*adj*	disgraceful, horrible, monstrous, offensive, shocking, unspeakable, wicked
		opposites: acceptable, reasonable
outside	*adj*	exterior, external, outdoor, outer, outward, surface
		opposites: central, inside, interior

outstanding	*adj*	eminent, excellent, extraordinary, great, important, notable, remarkable, special, superior
		opposites: ordinary, unexceptional
overcome	*verb*	beat, conquer, crush, defeat, master, overpower, overthrow, subdue, vanquish
		opposites: be defeated by, succumb
overlook	*verb*	1 ignore, miss, neglect, omit, pass
		opposites: notice, take account of
		2 excuse, forgive, pardon
		opposites: penalise, punish
overthrow	*verb*	conquer, defeat, depose, overpower, subdue, topple, vanquish
		opposites: install, reinstate, restore to power
own	*verb*	have, hold, keep, possess, retain
		opposites: give away, give up, release

P

pacify	*verb*	appease, calm, humour, placate, quieten, soothe
		opposites: aggravate, annoy, stir up
pack	*noun*	band, collection, crowd, flock, group, mob, set
		opposites: individual, single person
	verb	bundle, fill, load, store, stuff, thrust, wedge
		opposites: loosen, unpack
pad	*verb*	lope, move, run, step lightly, tread, trudge, walk
pain	*noun*	ache, agony, discomfort, heartache, hurt, irritation, soreness, suffering, torment, torture, twinge
		opposites: contentment, enjoyment, pleasure
painful	*adj*	1 aching, agonising, excruciating, sore, tender, unpleasant
		opposite: painless
		2 difficult, distasteful, distressing, hard, troublesome
		opposites: easy, simple
pair	*noun*	brace, couple, duo, match, twosome
pale	*adj*	ashen, bloodless, colourless, light, pasty, washed-out, white, whitish
		opposites: bright, high-coloured, ruddy
pamper	*verb*	baby, coddle, cosset, fondle, humour, indulge, mother, pet, spoil
		opposites: ill-treat, neglect
pandemonium	*noun*	chaos, confusion, din, hubbub, hullabaloo, racket, rumpus, turmoil, uproar
		opposites: peace, quiet, tranquillity
panic	*noun*	agitation, alarm, consternation, fear, fright, hysteria, terror
		opposites: calm, composure, peace
parade	*verb*	1 march, strut, swagger
		opposite: slouch

2 display, exhibit, make a show of, show
opposites: conceal, cover

parallel	*adj*	alongside, corresponding, equidistant, like, matching, resembling, similar *opposites:* divergent, separate
parched	*adj*	arid, dehydrated, dried up, dry, shrivelled, thirsty *opposites:* damp, well-watered, wet
pardon	*verb*	absolve, acquit, excuse, forgive, let off, overlook, reprieve *opposites:* condemn, lock up
part	*noun*	bit, branch, component, division, element, fragment, ingredient, piece, portion, section, segment, slice, unit *opposites:* totality, whole
particular	*adj*	detailed, distinct, peculiar, precise, singular, specific, unique, unusual *opposite:* general
partner	*noun*	accomplice, ally, colleague, companion, helper, husband, mate, wife *opposites:* competitor, enemy, rival
party	*noun*	1 celebration, entertainment, festivity, function, get-together, jollification, social 2 band, company, gang, gathering, group, squad, team
pass	*verb*	1 go, go by, go past, move, outdistance, overtake, proceed *opposites:* follow, succeed 2 convey, deliver, give, hand, hand over, send, throw, transfer *opposites:* receive, take 3 accept, approve, authorise, ratify, sanction *opposites:* fail, forbid

passable   *adj*   acceptable, adequate, average, fair, middling, moderate, presentable

opposites: above average, below average, exceptional, unacceptable

passage   *noun*   1 access, avenue, channel, corridor, crossing, hall, lane, opening, passageway, road, thoroughfare, way

opposites: barrier, blockage

2 communication, excerpt, paragraph, piece, portion, section, text, verse

passionate   *adj*   1 emotional, enthusiastic, fiery, hot-headed, hot-tempered, wild, zealous

opposites: calm, laid-back, uncommitted, unexcited

2 amorous, ardent, loving, sensual, warm

opposites: frigid, unloving

pastime   *noun*   activity, amusement, entertainment, game, hobby, recreation, relaxation, sport

patch   *verb*   cover, fix, mend, reinforce, repair, sew up, stitch

patient   *adj*   calm, long-suffering, quiet, self-controlled, serene, understanding

opposites: impatient, intolerant

patrol   *verb*   guard, inspect, police, walk round

pattern   *noun*   1 arrangement, design, example, method, model, plan, standard, type

2 decoration, ornament, ornamentation

pause   *verb*   delay, discontinue, halt, hesitate, interrupt, stop, take a break, wait

opposites: carry on, continue, proceed

noun   break, breather, gap, hesitation, interval, rest, wait

peaceful	*adj*	calm, gentle, placid, restful, still, tranquil, undisturbed
		opposites: agitated, disturbed, troubled
peculiar	*adj*	1 abnormal, bizarre, eccentric, extraordinary, quaint, queer, strange, weird
		opposites: commonplace, normal, ordinary
		2 distinctive, individual, particular, personal, special, unique
		opposites: general, uncharacteristic
penalty	*noun*	fine, forfeit, handicap, price, punishment
		opposites: prize, reward
penetrate	*verb*	enter, get through to, infiltrate, pierce, stab, strike into
people	*noun*	citizens, community, folk, general public, human beings, masses, multitude, nation, persons, population
perfect	*adj*	complete, excellent, faultless, flawless, ideal, spot-on, superb, true, untarnished, whole
		opposites: flawed, imperfect, incomplete
perform	*verb*	accomplish, bring about, carry out, do, effect, produce, transact
		opposites: fail to do, omit
perfume	*noun*	aroma, bouquet, fragrance, odour, scent
peril	*noun*	danger, menace, risk, threat
		opposites: safety, security
perish	*verb*	collapse, decay, die, disappear, disintegrate, pass away, rot, wither
		opposites: exist, endure, live, survive
permanent	*adj*	eternal, everlasting, long-lasting, unchanging
		opposites: brief, fleeting, temporary
permit	*noun*	authorisation, licence, pass, passport, permission, visa

per<u>mit</u>	*verb*	allow, authorise, enable, give leave, grant, let
		opposites: forbid, refuse
perplexed	*adj*	baffled, bewildered, confused, muddled, mystified, puzzled
		opposites: aware, knowing
persecute	*verb*	harass, hound, ill-treat, molest, oppress, pester, tease, torment, torture
		opposites: humour, pamper, protect
persevere	*verb*	carry on, continue, persist, plug away, remain, stand firm, stick at (something)
		opposites: give in, give up, surrender, yield
persist	*verb*	carry on, continue, hang on, keep going, last, persevere, stick at (something)
		opposites: discontinue, give up, stop
person	*noun*	being, body, character, human being, individual
personal	*adj*	individual, own, particular, private, special
		opposites: general, public, universal
persuade	*verb*	bring round, coax, convert, convince, influence, prevail upon, satisfy, talk into, win over
		opposites: discourage, dissuade, put off
pest	*noun*	annoyance, bother, irritation, nuisance, scourge
pester	*verb*	annoy, bother, disturb, get at, hassle, pick on, torment
		opposites: delight, please
petty	*adj*	1 grudging, mean, shabby, small-minded
		opposites: generous, large-hearted
		2 insignificant, negligible, small, trifling, unimportant
		opposites: important, significant
phenomenal	*adj*	exceptional, uncommon, unusual, wonderful
		opposites: ordinary, unexceptional

pick	*verb*	1 choose, decide on, opt for, select, single out
		opposites: ignore, reject
		2 gather, harvest, pluck
		opposites: disperse, scatter, spread
picture	*noun*	drawing, illustration, likeness, painting, photograph, sketch
piece	*noun*	bit, component, element, fraction, fragment, part, portion, scrap, slice
		opposites: complete amount, total, whole
pierce	*verb*	bore, drill, enter, impale, penetrate, prick, puncture, stab, wound
pile	*noun*	collection, heap, hoard, mound, stockpile
	verb	build up, collect, gather, heap, pack, store
		opposites: disperse, scatter, spread
pinch	*verb*	crush, nip, press, squeeze, tweak
pitch	*verb*	cast, fling, heave, hurl, sling, throw, toss
	noun	1 angle, gradient, incline, slope, steepness
		opposites: flat, horizontal
		2 ground, park, playing-field, sports field
pitiful	*adj*	contemptible, heart-breaking, hopeless, miserable, pathetic, sad, wretched
		opposites: admirable, cheerful, contented
pity	*noun*	compassion, kindness, mercy, sympathy, tenderness, understanding
		opposites: cruelty, scorn
place	*noun*	area, district, locality, location, neighbourhood, space, spot, vicinity
	verb	arrange, deposit, group, lay, put, set
		opposites: displace, move, transfer
plague	*noun*	blight, contagion, disease, epidemic, pestilence

plain	*adj*	1 bare, basic, ordinary, simple, uncomplicated, unpretentious
		opposites: complicated, elaborate, ornamented, ostentatious, rich
		2 apparent, clear, distinct, obvious, unmistakeable, visible
		opposites: dubious, unclear, obscure
plan	*noun*	1 blueprint, design, layout, map, sketch
		2 idea, method, plot, programme, project, scheme, strategy, system
plant	*noun*	bush, flower, herb, shrub, weed
play	*verb*	1 fool around, frolic, sport
		opposite: be serious
		2 act, perform
	noun	1 activity, amusement, entertainment, fun, game, pastime, recreation
		opposites: employment, work
		2 drama, performance, production, theatricals
plead	*verb*	ask, beg, beseech, implore, request
pleasant	*adj*	agreeable, amusing, cheery, delightful, enjoyable, friendly, likeable, pleasing, satisfying
		opposites: distasteful, nasty, unpleasant
please	*verb*	amuse, delight, entertain, humour, indulge
		opposites: anger, displease, upset
plentiful	*adj*	abundant, copious, fruitful, lavish
		opposites: scanty, scarce
plot	*noun*	1 conspiracy, plan, scheme
		2 narrative, outline, story, story-line
pluck	*verb*	collect, gather, harvest, pick, pull off, snatch, tug
		opposites: put back, return

plump   *adj*   beefy, buxom, fat, obese, stout

                         opposites: skinny, thin

plunge   *verb*   dive, drop, fall, go down, sink, submerge, tumble

                         opposites: ascend, emerge, rise up

point   *verb*   aim, direct, draw attention to, indicate, show, signal

                   noun   1 end, tip

                            2 aim, design, intention, objective, purpose, use

                            3 feature, location, place, position, site, spot

poke   *verb*   dig, hit, jab, nudge, prod, stab, thrust

polish   *verb*   brush up, improve, rub up, shine, smooth

                         opposites: dull down, tarnish

polite   *adj*   civil, considerate, courteous, mannerly, respectful,
                            well-mannered

                         opposites: discourteous, impolite, rude, ungracious

poor   *adj*   1 badly off, hard up, needy, penniless,
                            poverty-stricken

                            opposites: rich, wealthy, well off

                            2 inadequate, inferior, insufficient, miserable, pitiable

                            opposites: adequate, good, superior

popular   *adj*   in demand, in favour, liked, well-liked

                         opposites: disliked, unpopular

portion   *noun*   bit, fragment, helping, morsel, part, piece, scrap,
                            segment, slice

                         opposites: all, full amount, whole

position   *noun*   1 location, point, site, spot, whereabouts

                            2 circumstances, employment, job, occupation, post,
                            situation

                            3 arrangement, attitude, posture, stature

                            4 belief, opinion, outlook, point of view, stance,
                            viewpoint

positive   *adj*   assertive, certain, clear, confident, firm, forceful, hopeful, thorough
opposites: indecisive, negative, uncertain

possess   *verb*   have, hold, obtain, occupy, seize, take over
opposites: give up, release, relinquish

possible   *adj*   attainable, feasible, imaginable, viable, workable
opposites: impossible, not feasible

post   *noun*   1 column, pillar, pole, shaft, strut, support

2 employment, job, office, position

3 correspondence, letters, mail

postpone   *verb*   delay, hold over, put back, put off, shelve, suspend
opposites: act on, advance, bring forward

poverty   *noun*   hardship, lack, need, penury, scarcity, shortage, want
opposites: affluence, riches, wealth

power   *noun*   1 authority, command, control, influence, mastery, supremacy
opposites: inability, powerlessness

2 force, might, muscle, strength, vigour
opposite: weakness

practical   *adj*   down-to-earth, efficient, matter-of-fact, ordinary, realistic, sensible, skilled
opposites: impractical, ineffective

practice   *noun*   1 drill, exercise, experience, training, work, work-out

2 custom, habit, method, policy, procedure, routine, system

practise   *verb*   drill, rehearse, train

praise   *verb*   applaud, commend, compliment, congratulate, flatter, honour, speak well of
opposites: criticise, revile

precious	*adj*	beloved, choice, favourite, invaluable, loved, priceless, prized, rare, valuable, valued
		opposites: despised, of no account, unloved, unvalued
precise	*adj*	accurate, careful, exact, meticulous, rigid, specific, strict
		opposites: approximate, imprecise, rough-and-ready
predictable	*adj*	expected, foreseeable, likely, probable
		opposites: uncertain, unpredictable
prefer	*verb*	choose, incline towards, like better, pick, select
		opposites: refuse, regret, turn down
prejudice	*noun*	bias, bigotry, intolerance, unfairness
		opposites: fairness, tolerance
premature	*adj*	early, hasty, undeveloped, unripe
		opposites: late, tardy
prepare	*verb*	arrange, assemble, develop, form, make ready
		opposites: disarrange, dismantle
preposterous	*adj*	absurd, foolish, insane, laughable, ridiculous, unthinkable
		opposites: reasonable, sensible
present	*noun*	donation, gift, offer
	adj	at hand, available, here, near, ready, to hand
		opposites: absent, away, past
present	*verb*	1 award, donate, give, hand over, hold out, offer, show
		opposites: take back, withdraw
		2 announce, introduce
preserve	*verb*	defend, guard, keep, look after, protect, save, shield
		opposites: destroy, ruin
press	*verb*	crush, force down, jam, push, squeeze
pressure	*noun*	burden, demands, difficulty, strain, stress, weight

presume	*verb*	assume, believe, count on, rely on, suppose, take for granted, think, trust
		opposites: disbelieve, doubt, ignore
pretend	*verb*	act, claim, feign, make believe, suppose
pretty	*adj*	attractive, beautiful, good-looking, lovely, pleasing
		opposites: plain, ugly, unattractive
prevent	*verb*	block, check, hamper, hinder, obstruct, stop
		opposites: allow, assist, cause, help
previous	*adj*	earlier, former, past, prior, sometime
		opposite: later
price	*noun*	cost, expense, fee, payment, value, worth
priceless	*adj*	costly, expensive, invaluable, precious, prized, rare
		opposites: cheap, valueless, worthless
pride	*noun*	1 arrogance, conceit, self-importance, vanity
		opposite: humility
		2 dignity, honour, satisfaction, self-esteem
		opposites: low self-esteem, poor self-image
primitive	*adj*	earliest, first, original, primeval, undeveloped
		opposites: advanced, developed
principal	*adj*	chief, first, foremost, leading, main
		opposites: least, lesser, minor
	noun	chief, head, headteacher, leader, master
		opposites: servant, underling
principle	*noun*	1 honesty, honour, integrity, morality, truth
		2 belief, conviction, rule
prison	*noun*	cage, cell, clink, dungeon, gaol / jail
prisoner	*noun*	captive, convict, detainee, hostage, inmate
		opposites: escapee, fugitive
private	*adj*	confidential, intimate, own, personal, secret
		opposites: open, public

prize	*noun*	award, goal, reward, trophy, winnings
	adj	best, excellent, first-rate, outstanding, top
		opposite: second-rate
probably	*adv*	likely, maybe, most likely, perhaps, possibly
problem	*noun*	complication, dilemma, puzzle, quandary, trouble
		opposites: answer, solution
proceed	*verb*	advance, begin, carry on, continue, go on, move forward, press on, start
		opposites: go back, retreat, return, stop
produce	*verb*	1 bring forth, deliver, give, offer, present, put forward, show, yield
		opposites: hold back, keep, retain
		2 cause, construct, make, supply
		opposite: prevent
profession	*noun*	career, employment, job, occupation
professional	*adj*	expert, masterly, skilled, trained
		opposites: amateur, slapdash, unprofessional
profit	*noun*	1 advantage, benefit, gain, use
		opposite: disadvantage
		2 earnings, interest, proceeds, receipts, return, winnings
		opposite: loss
programme	*noun*	agenda, list, plan, project, scheme
progress	*noun*	advancement, betterment, development, gain, improvement, promotion
		opposites: deterioration, worsening
prohibited	*adj*	banned, disallowed, forbidden, not allowed
		opposites: allowed, permitted
project	*noun*	enterprise, idea, plan, programme, proposal, task, undertaking

promise	*verb*	give an undertaking, guarantee, pledge, suggest, swear, vow
	noun	commitment, guarantee, oath, pledge, vow, word of honour
promising	*adj*	encouraging, favourable, hopeful, likely, up-and-coming
		opposites: hopeless, unpromising
prompt	*adj*	early, instant, on time, punctual, quick, rapid, speedy, timely
		opposites: late, slow
proper	*adj*	correct, fitting, legitimate, precise, right, suitable
		opposites: improper, unsuited, wrong
propose	*verb*	put forward, recommend, suggest
prosper	*verb*	become rich, do well, flourish, grow rich, succeed, thrive
		opposites: decline, do badly, fail
protect	*verb*	care for, defend, guard, look after, shelter, shield, support, watch over
		opposites: attack, threaten
pro<u>test</u>	*noun*	complaint, dissent, objection, outcry
		opposites: acceptance, agreement
pro<u>test</u>	*verb*	complain, disagree, object, oppose
		opposites: accept, support
proud	*adj*	1 arrogant, conceited, overbearing, vain
		opposites: humble, modest
		2 glorious, great, magnificent, noble, satisfying, splendid
		opposites: mean, undignified
prove	*verb*	bear out, confirm, demonstrate, establish, show
		opposite: disprove
provide	*verb*	give, produce, serve, supply
		opposites: remove, take

prowl	*verb*	creep, hunt, roam, search, slink, stalk
prudent	*adj*	careful, cautious, sensible, shrewd, wary
		opposites: imprudent, rash, unwise
public	*adj*	common, known, obvious, open, well-known
		opposites: hidden, private
	noun	community, people, society
publish	*verb*	broadcast, circulate, disclose, print, publicise, reveal
		opposite: keep secret
pull	*verb*	drag, draw out, extract, haul, pluck, stretch, tug, wrench
		opposites: push, repel
punish	*verb*	beat, harm, hurt, injure, rough up, trounce
pupil	*noun*	learner, novice, scholar, schoolboy, schoolgirl
		opposites: instructor, teacher
purchase	*verb*	acquire, buy, obtain, pay for
		opposite: sell
pure	*adj*	1 clean, clear, genuine, spotless, unmixed, untainted
		opposites: polluted, tainted
		2 blameless, innocent, perfect, virtuous
		opposites: impure, sinful
purify	*verb*	clean, cleanse, filter, wash
		opposites: contaminate, defile, pollute
purpose	*noun*	aim, design, end, goal, intention, motive, reason, use
pursue	*verb*	chase, follow, go for, hunt, shadow, trail
		opposites: avoid, shun
push	*verb*	1 poke, prod, propel, shoulder, shove, thrust
		opposites: pull, tug
		2 egg on, encourage, persuade, spur
		opposites: discourage, hamper, hinder
puzzle	*verb*	baffle, bewilder, confuse, mystify, stump
		opposites: clear up, make plain

Q

quaint	*adj*	curious, eccentric, odd, queer, strange, unusual, weird
		opposites: normal, ordinary
qualified	*adj*	capable, competent, experienced, knowledgeable, skilled, trained
		opposites: unqualified, unskilled
quality	*noun*	1 distinction, excellence, merit, superiority, talent, value, worth
		opposites: inferiority, lack of distinction, lack of talent
		2 aspect, characteristic, feature, grade, nature, tone
quandary	*noun*	difficulty, dilemma, fix, jam
quantity	*noun*	amount, capacity, magnitude, mass, number, volume
quarrel	*noun*	argument, conflict, disagreement, dispute, feud, fight, row, strife
		opposites: agreement, harmony
quarrelsome	*adj*	argumentative, belligerent, cross, ill-tempered, irritable, truculent
		opposites: easygoing, peaceable, placid
quash	*verb*	cancel, mollify, overrule, reverse, squash, suppress
		opposites: confirm, justify
queer	*adj*	1 curious, mysterious, outlandish, odd, peculiar, strange, uncommon, unusual, weird
		opposites: common, ordinary, normal, usual
		2 dizzy, giddy, ill, queasy, unwell
		opposites: fit, well
quench	*verb*	1 damp down, extinguish, put out, snuff out
		opposites: ignite, light, set fire to
		2 satisfy, slake (your thirst)
quest	*noun*	adventure, crusade, exploration, journey, mission, pilgrimage, search, undertaking, voyage

question	*verb*	ask, challenge, doubt, enquire, examine, interrogate, interview, probe, quiz
		opposites: answer, explain, inform, tell
questionable	*adj*	doubtful, dubious, shady, suspect, suspicious, unreliable
		opposites: certain, undoubted
quick	*adj*	1 agile, brisk, fast, lively, nimble, nippy, prompt, rapid, swift
		opposites: dull, slow
		2 alive, eager, quick-witted, smart
		opposites: slow on the uptake, stupid, unintelligent
quiet	*adj*	1 calm, gentle, placid, tranquil
		opposites: agitated, rash
		2 hushed, noiseless, silent, soft, subdued, without noise
		opposites: loud, noisy
quit	*verb*	abandon, cease, end, give up, leave, retire, stop
		opposites: begin, continue
quiver	*verb*	flicker, flutter, pulsate, shake, shiver, shudder, tremble, vibrate
quiz	*verb*	cross-examine, examine, grill, interrogate, investigate, question
		opposites: answer, explain, respond
quotation	*noun*	1 extract, passage, quote, reference
		2 charge, cost, estimate, price, quote, rate

R

race	*verb*	dart, dash, gallop, hasten, run, rush, speed, sprint *opposites:* linger, loiter, slow down, stroll
racket	*noun*	1 clamour, commotion, din, disturbance, noise, uproar *opposites:* quiet, silence, tranquillity
		2 con, deception, fiddle, fraud, trick *opposites:* honest dealings, straight dealings
rage	*noun*	anger, frenzy, fury, passion, violence, wrath *opposites:* calm, composure
ragged	*adj*	broken, disorganised, frayed, irregular, jagged, uneven *opposites:* smooth, straight
raid	*noun*	attack, invasion, onslaught
	verb	attack, invade, plunder, ransack *opposites:* defend, protect
raise	*verb*	1 hoist, lift, uplift *opposites:* drop, lay down, put down
		2 arouse, boost, excite, grow, increase, strengthen *opposites:* deflate, depress, suppress
		3 assemble, build, construct, erect *opposites:* destroy, flatten
rambling	*adj*	disjointed, incoherent, long-winded, straggling, wordy *opposites:* concise, direct, to the point
random	*adj*	aimless, casual, haphazard, unplanned *opposites:* deliberate, planned
range	*noun*	extent, limits, radius, span, variety
rank	*noun*	class, category, grade, position, status
rapid	*adj*	fast, hasty, hurried, prompt, quick, speedy, swift *opposites:* leisurely, slow, sluggish
rash	*adj*	foolhardy, hasty, hot-headed, impulsive, reckless, thoughtless *opposites:* careful, cautious, thoughtful

rate	*noun*	1 charge, cost, dues, fee, price, reckoning, value
		2 pace, speed, velocity
rattle	*verb*	1 clank, clatter
		2 confuse, fluster, perturb, upset
		opposites: calm, compose, put at ease
ravenous	*adj*	famished, hungry, starving
		opposites: satisfied, well-fed
raw	*adj*	1 fresh, green, uncooked
		opposite: cooked
		2 inexperienced, untrained, untried
		opposites: experienced, skilled
		3 biting, chilly, freezing, very cold
		opposites: pleasant, warm
reach	*verb*	1 arrive at, come to, get to, land at
		2 contact, touch
ready	*adj*	available, convenient, handy, near, on tap, prepared
		opposites: unprepared, unready
real	*adj*	authentic, genuine, true, valid
		opposites: imaginary, unreal
realise	*verb*	1 appreciate, comprehend, imagine, recognise, understand
		opposites: be unaware of, misunderstand
		2 achieve, complete, implement, make
		opposites: botch, fail to do
rear	*noun*	back, end, hindquarter, stern, tail
		opposites: front, head
reason	*noun*	1 cause, explanation, intention, motive
		2 common sense, intellect, judgement, mind, understanding, wisdom

reasonable	*adj*	believable, fair, justifiable, logical, moderate, sensible
		opposites: crazy, irrational, unreasonable, unwise
rebel	*verb*	defy, disobey, mutiny, resist, turn against
		opposites: follow, obey, support
rebellion	*noun*	disobedience, mutiny, resistance, revolt, rising, uprising
		opposites: obedience, support
recall	*verb*	1 recollect, remember
		opposite: forget
		2 call back
		opposite: send out
receive	*verb*	accept, acquire, collect, gather, get, obtain, take
		opposites: hand over, give
recent	*adj*	latest, new, modern, up-to-date
		opposites: dated, old, out-of-date
recite	*verb*	deliver, narrate, perform, speak, tell
reckless	*adj*	careless, foolhardy, hasty, rash, thoughtless
		opposites: calculating, careful, cautious
recline	*verb*	lean, lie, lounge, rest, sprawl, stretch out
		opposites: arise, sit up, stand up
recognise	*verb*	1 identify, know, notice, remember, see, spot, understand
		opposites: fail to recognise, miss, overlook
		2 acknowledge, admit, concede, confess
		opposites: deny, reject
recommend	*verb*	advise, approve, commend, propose, suggest, vouch for
		opposites: disapprove, veto
record	*noun*	1 account, entry, minute, report, written account
		2 best achievement, best performance

recover	*verb*	1 heal, improve, mend, pick up, pull through, revive
		opposites: decline, get worse, relapse
		2 recapture, reclaim, regain, repossess, retrieve
		opposites: forfeit, give up, lose
recreation	*noun*	amusement, entertainment, exercise, fun, leisure activity, play, pleasure, relaxation, sport
		opposites: employment, work
red	*adj*	blood red, crimson, maroon, ruby, scarlet, vermilion
reduce	*verb*	contract, curtail, cut, decrease, dilute, trim, weaken
		opposites: boost, fatten, increase
reflect	*verb*	1 mirror, reproduce, reveal, show
		2 consider, contemplate, ponder, think
reform	*verb*	improve, mend, rectify, remodel, repair, restore
refresh	*verb*	cool, freshen, renew, restore, revive, stimulate
		opposites: exhaust, tire
refuse	*verb*	decline, deny, reject, repudiate, spurn, withhold
		opposites: accept, allow
regard	*noun*	consideration, esteem, love, notice, reputation, sympathy
		opposites: contempt, disapproval, dislike
region	*noun*	area, district, land, province, sector, territory, zone
register	*noun*	catalogue, file, list, log, record, roll, schedule
regret	*verb*	apologise, be sorry, lament, grieve, repent
		opposites: be glad, rejoice
regular	*adj*	1 constant, even, rhythmic, steady, unvarying
		opposites: irregular, sporadic
		2 common, everyday, normal, ordinary, standard, typical
		opposites: odd, unconventional, unusual
rehearse	*verb*	drill, practise, prepare, study, train

reject	*verb*	deny, disallow, exclude, refuse, repudiate, spurn
		opposites: accept, select
relate	*verb*	describe, narrate, recite, recount, report, tell
relax	*verb*	ease, lessen, loosen, reduce, relieve, rest, unwind, weaken
		opposites: intensify, tighten
release	*verb*	deliver, drop, free, unloose, untie
		opposites: check, detain, hold, keep
reliable	*adj*	dependable, faithful, responsible, safe, solid, sure, trustworthy
		opposites: doubtful, suspect, unreliable, untrustworthy
relieve	*verb*	assist, comfort, console, ease, free, help, soothe, support
		opposites: aggravate, intensify
reluctant	*adj*	disinclined, hesitant, loath, unenthusiastic, unwilling
		opposites: eager, keen, willing
remain	*verb*	continue, endure, last, linger, stand, stay, survive, wait
		opposites: depart, go, leave
remark	*noun*	comment, mention, observation, statement, thought, utterance, word
remarkable	*adj*	amazing, exceptional, extraordinary, outstanding, uncommon, unusual
		opposites: average, commonplace, ordinary
remember	*verb*	recall, recollect, think back
		opposite: forget
remove	*verb*	displace, eject, extract, oust, take away, take out
		opposites: put back, replace, return
renew	*verb*	modernise, overhaul, refit, repair, replace, restore, transform
repair	*verb*	fix, heal, make good, mend, rectify, restore

opposites: break, damage, destroy

repay	*verb*	1 avenge, get even with, retaliate, revenge
		2 pay back, refund, return, reward
repeat	*verb*	duplicate, redo, rehearse, restate, reproduce, retell
replace	*verb*	1 follow, oust, substitute, supersede
		2 put back, return
reply	*verb*	answer, respond, retaliate, retort
report	*noun*	account, information, message, news, record, rumour, statement, summary
reproduce	*verb*	1 breed, bring forth young, give birth
		2 copy, duplicate, mirror, repeat, represent
require	*verb*	ask, command, compel, demand, direct, instruct, order, want
rescue	*verb*	free, liberate, ransom, redeem, release, save
		opposites: capture, imprison
reserve	*verb*	1 book, secure
		2 hoard, keep, put by, retain, store
		opposite: use up
residence	*noun*	abode, dwelling, home, house, quarters
resign	*verb*	abdicate, leave, quit, relinquish, stand down, surrender, vacate
		opposites: join, remain, stay
resist	*verb*	confront, defy, fight back, oppose, struggle against, withstand
		opposites: accept, give in, submit
resourceful	*adj*	able, capable, clever, imaginative, quick-witted
		opposites: dull, slow-witted, unimaginative
resources	*noun*	assets, capital, funds, materials, means, money, reserves, supplies
		opposites: debts, liabilities

respect	*noun*	admiration, esteem, honour, regard, reverence
		opposites: contempt, disrespect
	verb	admire, appreciate, heed, look up to, revere, value
		opposites: despise, scorn
respectable	*adj*	1 clean-living, decent, good, honest, upright, worthy
		opposites: bad, disreputable
		2 fair, passable, reasonable, sizeable
		opposites: excessive, huge, immense, small, unacceptable
responsible	*adj*	adult, dependable, level-headed, mature, reliable, sensible, trustworthy
		opposites: irresponsible, unreliable
restful	*adj*	calm, comfortable, peaceful, relaxed, relaxing, soothing, undisturbed
		opposites: disturbed, upsetting
restless	*adj*	anxious, edgy, nervous, troubled, uneasy, unsettled
		opposites: calm, relaxed
restore	*verb*	fix, mend, rebuild, reconstruct, renew, repair, replace, return
restrain	*verb*	arrest, control, hamper, hinder, hold back, imprison, prevent, subdue
		opposites: encourage, free, let loose
restrict	*verb*	hamper, impede, limit, restrain
		opposites: broaden, encourage, free
result	*noun*	conclusion, decision, effect, end, outcome, upshot
		opposites: beginning, cause
resume	*verb*	continue, pick up, proceed, reopen, restart, take-up
		opposites: cease, leave off, stop
retain	*verb*	keep, maintain, preserve, reserve, save
		opposites: release, spend, use up

retire	*verb*	depart, give up work, leave
		opposites: continue working, stay
retreat	*verb*	depart, go back, leave, quit, retire, turn tail
		opposites: advance, attack
return	*verb*	1 give back, replace, restore, send back
		opposites: keep, retain, take
		2 come back, go back, reappear
		opposites: go, leave, quit
	noun	1 benefit, compensation, interest, profit, reward
		opposites: expenses, loss, payment, outgoings
		2 comeback, reappearance, rebound, reply, response
		opposite: disappearance
reveal	*verb*	disclose, display, expose, publish, show, tell, uncover
		opposites: conceal, hide
reverse	*verb*	1 backtrack, go backwards, move backwards
		opposites: advance, go forward
		2 alter, overrule, repeal, retract, upset
		opposites: confirm, enforce, maintain
revise	*verb*	alter, change, modify, reconsider, re-examine, review, rewrite
revive	*verb*	bring back to life, rekindle, renew, restore, rouse
		opposites: kill, suppress
revolting	*adj*	abominable, disgusting, horrible, loathsome, offensive, repulsive
		opposites: attractive, pleasant
revolve	*verb*	circle, orbit, rotate, spin, turn, wheel, whirl
reward	*noun*	compensation, gain, payment, prize, profit, remuneration, return, wages
		opposites: penalty, punishment

rich	*adj*	1 affluent, expensive, prosperous, wealthy
		opposites: needy, poor
		2 full, juicy, lavish, luscious, succulent, sumptuous
		opposites: plain, simple, tasteless
		3 bright, deep, vivid
		opposites: dull, unexciting
riddle	*noun*	conundrum, mystery, poser, problem, puzzle
ridicule	*verb*	jeer at, mock, scoff at, send up, taunt
		opposites: commend, praise
	noun	derision, jeering, mockery, sarcasm, scorn, sneering
		opposites: commendation, praise
ridiculous	*adj*	absurd, comical, foolish, laughable, ludicrous, nonsensical, outrageous, stupid
		opposites: logical, reasonable, sensible
right	*adj*	1 accurate, correct, genuine, proper, true
		opposites: incorrect, wrong
		2 fair, good, honest, lawful, moral, rightful, satisfactory, virtuous
		opposites: dishonest, unlawful, wrong
rigid	*adj*	fixed, inflexible, set, stiff, strict, unbending
		opposites: flexible, pliant
ring	*noun*	1 band, circle, circuit, hoop, loop
		2 gang, group, organisation, syndicate
ripe	*adj*	full-grown, mature
		opposites: immature, unripe, young
rise	*verb*	ascend, climb, emerge, get up, go up, mount, soar, spring up, surface
		opposites: descend, fall, sink
risk	*noun*	chance, gamble, peril, possibility, uncertainty
		opposites: certainty, safety

rival	*noun*	adversary, antagonist, competitor, opponent
		opposites: associate, colleague
rob	*verb*	dispossess, hold up, plunder, raid, ransack, swindle
		opposites: give, provide
robust	*adj*	brawny, healthy, muscular, powerful, rough, strong
		opposites: unhealthy, weak
rogue	*noun*	cheat, crook, rascal, scoundrel, villain
		opposites: hero, saint
roll	*verb*	1 curl, revolve, rotate, spin, turn, twirl
		2 flatten, level, press, smooth
romantic	*adj*	loving, passionate, sentimental, starry-eyed, tender
		opposites: humdrum, unromantic
root	*noun*	beginning, cause, foundation, heart, origin, source, starting-point
rot	*verb*	decay, fester, go bad, perish, spoil
rotate	*verb*	pivot, reel, revolve, spin, swivel, turn, wheel
rough	*adj*	1 approximate, general, imprecise, vague
		opposites: accurate, exact, precise
		2 bristly, bushy, coarse, craggy, shaggy, tangled, unshaven
		opposites: sleek, smooth
		3 grating, harsh, husky, jarring, rasping, unmusical
		opposites: musical, soft, sweet-sounding
		4 coarse, ill-mannered, rude, tough, uncouth
		opposites: polite, well-mannered
		5 choppy, inclement, squally, stormy, violent, wild
		opposites: calm, settled

round	*adj*	1 ball-shaped, rounded, spherical
		opposite: flat
		2 circular, curved, ring-shaped
		opposite: straight
route	*noun*	course, direction, journey, path, road, way
routine	*noun*	custom, method, pattern, way
	adj	boring, customary, everyday, normal, ordinary, run-of-the-mill, standard
		opposites: exciting, unusual
row	*noun*	brawl, dispute, quarrel, rumpus, trouble
		opposites: agreement, peace
rub	*verb*	caress, massage, polish, shine, stroke, wipe
rubbish	*noun*	1 debris, garbage, litter, refuse, waste
		2 claptrap, drivel, nonsense, twaddle
		opposite: sense
ruin	*verb*	bankrupt, break, damage, demolish, overthrow, shatter, smash, wreck
		opposites: develop, improve, make good, restore
rumour	*noun*	gossip, hearsay, report, story, whisperings
		opposites: fact, truth
run	*verb*	1 dash, gallop, hasten, hurry, race, rush, sprint
		opposites: stay, stop, stroll, walk
		2 administer, control, direct, manage, oversee, supervise
		opposites: obey, serve
rush	*verb*	charge, dash, hurry, run, scurry, speed, sprint
		opposites: crawl, move slowly
ruthless	*adj*	callous, cruel, heartless, merciless, savage, unfeeling
		opposites: compassionate, merciful

S

sacred	*adj*	blessed, divine, heavenly, religious, sanctified, venerable
		opposites: earthly, profane
sacrifice	*verb*	abandon, give up, let go, lose, renounce, surrender
sad	*adj*	dejected, depressed, downcast, gloomy, joyless, miserable, tearful, unhappy
		opposites: cheerful, happy, pleased
safe	*adj*	1 all right, protected, secure, unharmed, unscathed
		opposites: at risk, exposed, in danger, vulnerable
		2 dependable, prudent, sound, sure, trustworthy
		opposites: harmful, unsure
sail	*verb*	cruise, float, navigate, put to sea, steer, weigh anchor
sane	*adj*	level-headed, in your right mind, lucid, rational, sensible, stable
		opposites: not all there, insane, irrational, unbalanced
sarcastic	*adj*	biting, cutting, mocking, scathing, sneering
satisfactory	*adj*	acceptable, average, fair, passable, sufficient
		opposites: inadequate, unacceptable, unsatisfactory
satisfy	*verb*	convince, delight, persuade, please, reassure, reward
		opposites: disappoint, displease, fail, frustrate
saunter	*verb*	amble, dally, dawdle, meander, ramble, roam, stroll, wander
		opposites: hurry, run, walk fast
savage	*adj*	brutal, cruel, ferocious, ruthless, uncivilised, vicious, wild
		opposites: civilised, gentle, humane
save	*verb*	1 collect, gather, hoard, keep, put aside, reserve, stash, store
		opposites: discard, spend, waste
		2 defend, free, guard, preserve, protect, rescue, shield
		opposite: expose

say	*verb*	express, pronounce, recite, remark, speak, state, tell, utter
scarce	*adj*	few, insufficient, rare, scanty, sparse, uncommon *opposites:* common, copious, plentiful
scare	*verb*	alarm, frighten, shock, startle, terrify *opposites:* calm, reassure
scatter	*verb*	disperse, fling, shower, sow, spread, sprinkle *opposites:* collect, concentrate
scene	*noun*	background, environment, landscape, place, setting, situation, spectacle, view
scent	*noun*	aroma, bouquet, fragrance, odour, perfume, smell *opposites:* stench, stink
scheme	*noun*	1 design, method, outline, pattern, plan, plot, programme, strategy, theory 2 conspiracy, dodge, plot, ruse, subterfuge
scornful	*adj*	contemptuous, insulting, mocking, sarcastic, sneering *opposites:* admiring, complimentary, respectful
scoundrel	*noun*	cheat, good-for-nothing, rascal, rat, rogue, villain
scramble	*verb*	clamber, climb, push, rush, scrabble, strive, struggle
scrap	*noun*	bit, fragment, part, piece, shred, sliver, trace
	verb	abandon, cancel, demolish, discard, drop, throw out, write off *opposites:* reinstate, restore
scratch	*verb*	claw out, graze, mark, score, scrape
	noun	blemish, graze, mark, scrape
scream	*verb*	cry, roar, screech, shriek, squeal, yell *opposite:* whisper
search	*verb*	explore, look for, probe, ransack
secret	*adj*	concealed, hidden, mysterious, private, unknown *opposites:* open, public

section	*noun*	1 fragment, part, piece, portion, slice
		2 department, division, sector
see	*verb*	catch sight of, glimpse, make out, notice, observe, picture, recognise, spot, view
seize	*verb*	capture, catch, confiscate, grab, grasp, grip, snatch, take
		opposites: give up, let go, release, relinquish
select	*verb*	choose, pick, prefer, single out
		opposites: pass over, reject
selfish	*adj*	greedy, mean, self-centred
		opposites: generous, unselfish
send	*verb*	deliver, dispatch, propel, shoot, transmit
		opposites: keep, take back
sensible	*adj*	level-headed, practical, reasonable, wise
		opposites: stupid, unreasonable
separate	*verb*	disconnect, divide, part, split up, uncouple
		opposites: join, put together
	adj	disconnected, distinct, divided, individual, particular, single, unconnected
		opposites: connected, joined
serious	*adj*	1 alarming, critical, dangerous, important, urgent, worrying
		opposites: non-serious, trivial, unimportant
		2 humourless, long-faced, severe, stern, unsmiling
		opposites: light-hearted, smiling
serve	*verb*	aid, assist, help, supply, work for
		opposites: command, order

set	*verb*	1 lay, place, position, put, stand
		opposites: displace, remove, uproot
		2 arrange, direct, fix up, schedule
		3 cake, congeal, gel, harden, solidify, stiffen, thicken
		opposites: liquefy, melt
settle	*verb*	1 alight, descend, drop, lower, sink
		opposites: arise, raise up, stand up
		2 arrange, decide, determine, fix, order
		opposites: disturb, upset
severe	*adj*	cruel, fierce, grim, harsh, stern, strict, violent
		opposites: kind, mild, sympathetic
shabby	*adj*	down-at-heel, poor, ragged, run-down, threadbare, worn
		opposites: smart, well-dressed
shake	*verb*	move, shudder, stir, tremble, twitch, vibrate, waggle, wave
shame	*noun*	disgrace, dishonour, embarrassment, stain, stigma
		opposites: distinction, honour, pride
shape	*noun*	appearance, aspect, figure, form, outline, profile, silhouette
	verb	construct, form, make, mould, plan
share	*verb*	distribute, divide, go halves, split
	noun	contribution, portion, ration
sharp	*adj*	1 cutting, keen, piercing, pointed
		opposites: blunt, dull-edged
		2 acute, burning, painful, severe, stinging
		opposites: dull, mild
		3 alert, clever, quick, shrewd, smart
		opposites: slow, stupid

shelter	*verb*	cover, defend, guard, harbour, keep safe, protect, shield
		opposite: expose
shield	*verb*	cover, defend, guard, protect, shelter
		opposites: expose, reveal, uncover
shine	*verb*	1 flash, gleam, glimmer, glisten, glow, sparkle
		2 do well, excel, stand out
		opposites: do badly, fail
shiver	*verb*	quiver, shake, shudder, tremble
shock	*verb*	horrify, jolt, stun, surprise, unsettle
		opposites: delight, please, reassure
short	*adj*	1 brief, concise, small, tiny
		opposites: big, large, long
		2 inadequate, limited, little, scarce
		opposites: ample, plentiful
shout	*verb*	bellow, call loudly, cry, roar, scream, yell
		opposite: whisper
show	*verb*	1 display, exhibit, illustrate, present, reveal
		opposites: conceal, hide
		2 demonstrate, explain, instruct, prove, teach
shrewd	*adj*	clever, cunning, intelligent, smart
		opposites: naive, silly, unintelligent
shrill	*adj*	ear-piercing, high-pitched, penetrating, piercing, sharp
		opposites: gentle, low, soft
shut	*verb*	bar, bolt, close, fasten, lock
		opposites: open, unlock
shy	*adj*	bashful, diffident, modest, nervous, timid, wary
		opposites: bold, confident
sick	*adj*	ill, indisposed, not well, queasy, unwell
		opposites: healthy, in good health, well

sign	*noun*	clue, hint, indication, signal, symptom, warning
significant	*adj*	important, meaningful, noteworthy, serious, vital
		opposites: insignificant, meaningless, unimportant
silent	*adj*	noiseless, quiet, speechless, tongue-tied, unspoken, wordless
		opposites: loud, noisy, talkative
silly	*adj*	foolish, idiotic, irrational, ridiculous, stupid
		opposites: intelligent, sensible, wise
simple	*adj*	1 easy, elementary, straightforward, uncomplicated
		opposites: difficult, hard
		2 basic, humble, modest, plain, unadorned
		opposites: complicated, fancy, ornamented
sincere	*adj*	candid, frank, honest, open, straightforward, truthful
		opposites: dishonest, false, insincere
sink	*verb*	1 descend, dip, disappear, droop, plunge, submerge
		opposites: float, rise
		2 decrease, diminish, dwindle, fade, fail, slip, weaken, worsen
		opposites: improve, increase, prosper
skilful	*adj*	clever, competent, expert, proficient, skilled, trained
		opposites: awkward, clumsy, untrained
slay	*verb*	assassinate, butcher, destroy, execute, kill, massacre, murder, slaughter
		opposites: defend, protect, spare
sleek	*adj*	1 glossy, shiny
		opposite: dull
		2 smooth, well-fed, well-groomed
		opposites: coarse, drab
sleep	*verb*	doze, drop off, slumber, snooze
		opposite: wake

slender	*adj*	1 lean, slim, thin, willowy
		opposites: fat, thick
		2 faint, little, narrow, slight, small
		opposites: great, large
slight	*adj*	insignificant, minor, modest, paltry, trivial, unimportant
		opposites: considerable, large, major, significant
slim	*adj*	lean, slender, slight, thin, trim
		opposites: fat, heavy-built
slip	*verb*	1 fall, stagger, stumble, trip
		2 blunder, make a mistake
slow	*adj*	delayed, leisurely, long-drawn-out, plodding, sluggish
		opposites: quick, speedy
sly	*adj*	cunning, devious, foxy, shifty, underhand, wily
		opposites: frank, honest, open
small	*adj*	1 diminutive, little, miniature, minute, tiny, undersized
		opposites: big, huge, large
		2 insignificant, limited, minor, modest, negligible, slight, unimportant
		opposites: impressive, significant
smart	*adj*	1 astute, bright, clever, intelligent, quick-witted, shrewd
		opposites: stupid, unintelligent
		2 elegant, fashionable, neat, stylish, tidy
		opposites: dowdy, down-at-heel, untidy
smell	*noun*	aroma, fragrance, odour, perfume, scent, stench, stink

smooth	*adj*	1 even, flat, level, unbroken, unwrinkled
		opposites: bumpy, irregular, rough, uneven
		2 calm, easy, flowing, pleasant, regular, soothing, unruffled, well-ordered
		opposites: coarse, harsh
snatch	*verb*	grab, grasp, grip, pluck, pull, seize, take
		opposites: give back, restore
sneer	*verb*	jeer, laugh at, look down on, mock, ridicule, scorn
		opposites: commend, praise
sob	*verb*	bawl, blubber, cry, moan, shed tears, weep
		opposite: laugh
sober	*adj*	1 clear-headed, lucid, not drunk
		opposites: drunk, tipsy
		2 calm, moderate, rational, serene, solemn, steady
		opposites: excited, intemperate, irrational
soft	*adj*	1 downy, feathery, flabby, spongy, supple, yielding
		opposites: hard, stiff, unbending
		2 delicate, easy, gentle, mild, smooth, tender
		opposites: hard, harsh
		3 low, quiet, whispered
		opposites: loud, noisy
solid	*adj*	firm, hard, not hollow, rigid
		opposites: empty, hollow
solitary	*adj*	alone, friendless, isolated, single, sole
		opposite: accompanied
soothe	*verb*	calm, comfort, ease, pacify, quiet, relieve
		opposites: anger, disturb, upset
sore	*adj*	hurting, painful, raw, smarting, tender
sorrow	*noun*	anguish, distress, grief, misery, sadness, trouble, unhappiness

		opposites: happiness, joy
sorry	*adj*	apologetic, guilt-ridden, miserable, regretful, repentant, wretched
		opposites: delighted, glad, pleased
sort	*noun*	group, kind, type, variety
sound	*noun*	1 din, noise, tone
		opposite: silence
		2 utterance, voice
	adj	complete, healthy, perfect, right, undamaged, uninjured, whole
		opposites: broken, damaged, unsound
sour	*adj*	1 acid, bitter, rancid, tart, vinegary
		opposites: sugary, sweet
		2 disagreeable, ill-natured, waspish
		opposites: agreeable, good-natured, likeable, pleasant
souvenir	*noun*	gift, keepsake, memento, reminder, token
space	*noun*	1 accommodation, room
		2 break, distance, gap, interval, period
spare	*adj*	additional, extra, leftover, remaining, surplus, unused
		opposites: necessary, needed
	verb	let off, pardon, release
		opposites: condemn, execute, kill
sparkle	*verb*	flash, glint, glisten, glitter, scintillate, twinkle
speak	*verb*	converse, discuss, express, mention, say, talk, tell, utter
special	*adj*	exceptional, important, uncommon, unique, unusual
		opposites: common, normal, ordinary, usual

speed	*noun*	acceleration, haste, hurry, quickness, rapidity, swiftness
		opposites: delay, slowness
spell	*noun*	1 charm, incantation, sorcery
		2 innings, period, stint, stretch, term, time
spill	*verb*	discharge, pour out, overflow, scatter
spin	*verb*	gyrate, reel, revolve, rotate, turn, twirl, twist, wheel, whirl
splendid	*adj*	admirable, brilliant, dazzling, excellent, glorious, magnificent, superb, wonderful
		opposites: drab, ordinary
spoil	*verb*	1 damage, deface, destroy, disfigure, injure, ruin, upset
		opposites: correct, improve, make better
		2 indulge, mollycoddle, pamper
		opposite: be strict with
spread	*verb*	1 broaden, expand, open out, sprawl, unfold, widen
		opposites: close up, contract
		2 cast, distribute, scatter, strew
spring	*verb*	bounce, jump, leap, shoot up, vault
squabble	*verb*	argue, dispute, fall out, fight, quarrel
		opposites: agree, cooperate
squeeze	*verb*	crush, cuddle, embrace, grip, hug, press, squash
		opposites: release, unfold
squirm	*verb*	fidget, move, twist, wiggle, wriggle, writhe
stab	*verb*	jab, knife, pierce, puncture, stick in, thrust
stain	*noun*	blemish, discolouration, mark, smudge, spot
stand	*verb*	1 arise, become upright, get to your feet, rise to your feet
		opposites: lie down, sit down

		2 bear, endure, put up with, stomach, suffer, take, tolerate, withstand
start	*verb*	begin, commence, initiate, set up *opposites:* end, finish
startle	*verb*	amaze, astonish, frighten, scare, shock, surprise *opposites:* calm, soothe
state	*verb*	declare, express, report, say
	noun	condition, mood, quality, situation
stay	*verb*	1 dwell, live, reside
		2 last, linger, remain, wait *opposites:* go, leave, quit
steady	*adj*	1 even, regular, rhythmic, unbroken, uniform, unvarying *opposites:* unsteady, wavering
		2 calm, dependable, level-headed, reliable, safe *opposites:* irrational, unreliable
steal	*verb*	embezzle, pilfer, poach, shoplift, snatch, take, thieve *opposites:* return, give back
stern	*adj*	forbidding, frowning, grim, harsh, serious, strict, unsmiling *opposites:* easygoing, mild, pleasant
stiff	*adj*	1 firm, hard, inflexible, rigid, unbending, unyielding *opposites:* flexible, soft, yielding
		2 difficult, hard, severe, tough *opposite:* easy
		3 formal, pompous, standoffish, stubborn, wooden *opposites:* graceful, informal, suave
still	*adj*	calm, motionless, peaceful, placid, quiet, smooth, unruffled *opposites:* agitated, choppy, disturbed, noisy

stir	*verb*	agitate, beat, disturb, excite, mix

stop   *verb*   1   cease, conclude, end, finish, leave off, terminate
opposites: begin, start

2   bar, halt, intercept, interrupt, obstruct, prevent
opposites: allow, let go, release

3   linger, remain, rest, stay
opposites: go, leave, quit

store   *noun*   1   abundance, fund, plenty, stock, supply, wealth
opposites: scarcity, shortage

2   shop, warehouse

story   *noun*   anecdote, episode, fable, myth, narration, plot, tale, yarn

straight   *adj*   1   continuous, direct, even, level, unswerving
opposites: curved, indirect

2   decent, fair, honest, reliable, trustworthy, upright
opposites: dishonest, evasive

strange   *adj*   abnormal, bizarre, curious, extraordinary, odd, peculiar, uncanny, weird
opposites: common, familiar, ordinary

strict   *adj*   1   accurate, exact, faithful, perfect, true
opposites: approximate, flexible

2   firm, harsh, rigid, severe, stern, unsparing
opposites: easygoing, laid-back

strike   *verb*   attack, beat, hit, knock, slap, smack, thump, wallop

strive   *verb*   compete, fight, push oneself, strain, struggle, try
opposites: give in, give up, succumb

strong   *adj*   1   athletic, hardy, muscular, powerful, robust, sturdy, tough
opposites: puny, weak

2   concentrated, intense, undiluted
opposites: diluted, weak

stubborn	*adj*	headstrong, inflexible, obstinate, rigid, unbending, unyielding
		opposites: compliant, flexible
stumble	*verb*	blunder, fall, lurch, slip, stagger, stutter
stupid	*adj*	dense, dim, foolish, irresponsible, unintelligent
		opposites: alert, clever, sensible, wise
sturdy	*adj*	brawny, hardy, muscular, powerful, robust, solid, strong, well-made
		opposites: puny, weak
style	*noun*	1 custom, fashion, manner, method, type, variety
		2 elegance, flair, grace, sophistication, taste
		opposites: gracelessness, inelegance
subdue	*verb*	conquer, defeat, overcome, overpower, suppress, vanquish
		opposites: arouse, stir up
subject	*noun*	affair, business, issue, matter, question, theme, topic
submit	*verb*	agree, give in, knuckle under, succumb
		opposites: oppose, resist
succeed	*verb*	1 flourish, prosper, thrive, triumph
		opposites: decline, fail, lose
		2 follow, inherit, result
		opposites: go before, precede
sudden	*adj*	abrupt, hurried, prompt, rapid, startling, swift, unexpected, unforeseen
		opposites: expected, slow, well-considered
suffer	*verb*	bear, endure, put up with, stand, undergo
		opposites: avoid, overcome, resist
sufficient	*adj*	adequate, ample, copious, enough, plentiful
		opposites: inadequate, insufficient, not enough

suggestion	*noun*	1 plan, proposal, proposition, recommendation
		2 clue, hint, inkling, insinuation
suitable	*adj*	acceptable, appropriate, fitting, right, satisfactory
		opposites: inappropriate, unsuitable
superb	*adj*	admirable, excellent, first-rate, magnificent, marvellous, superior
		opposites: poor, second-rate
supply	*verb*	equip, furnish, give, produce, provide, yield
		opposites: remove, take
support	*verb*	aid, assist, back, encourage, foster, help, sustain, uphold
		opposites: contradict, oppose
suppose	*verb*	believe, consider, imagine, presume, think
		opposites: be certain, know
sure	*adj*	1 confident, positive, satisfied
		opposites: doubtful, unsure
		2 clear, definite, fixed, precise, reliable, unmistakeable
		opposites: indefinite, uncertain
surprise	*verb*	amaze, astonish, confuse, disconcert, startle
	noun	amazement, astonishment, bewilderment, jolt, shock, wonder
		opposites: composure, expectation
surrender	*verb*	give in, give up, relinquish, renounce, submit, succumb, yield
		opposites: fight on, resist
surround	*verb*	besiege, encircle, enclose, envelop, ring
suspicious	*adj*	1 doubtful, dubious, unbelieving
		opposites: trustful, unsuspecting

2 dodgy, fishy, peculiar, questionable, suspect
opposites: above board, innocent

sweet   *adj*   1 cloying, honeyed, sugary, syrupy
opposites: bitter, sour

2 affectionate, appealing, charming, delightful, gracious, likeable, unselfish
opposites: horrible, horrid, unpleasant

swell   *verb*   bulge, enlarge, expand, grow, increase, rise
opposites: contract, dwindle, shrink

swift   *adj*   fast, nimble, quick, rapid, speedy
opposites: slow, sluggish

sympathy   *noun*   comfort, compassion, fellow-feeling, pity, tenderness, understanding
opposites: coldness, indifference

systematic   *adj*   businesslike, efficient, logical, methodical, organised, well-planned
opposites: disorderly, disorganised, inefficient

T

tactful	*adj*	considerate, polite, sensitive, thoughtful
		opposites: clumsy, tactless
tactics	*noun*	approach, game plan, moves, plan, policy, procedure
take	*verb*	1 arrest, capture, catch, gather, grasp, pick, receive, remove, seize, steal
		opposites: give, hand over, release
		2 accompany, bring, carry, conduct, convey, guide, lead
		opposites: abandon, leave
talent	*noun*	ability, flair, gift, knack
		opposites: inability, weakness
talk	*verb*	chat, chatter, communicate, converse, gossip, say, speak, utter
talkative	*adj*	chatty, garrulous, long-winded, loquacious, wordy
		opposites: reserved, taciturn
tall	*adj*	big, giant, high, lanky, lofty, steep, towering
		opposites: low, short, squat
tame	*adj*	1 docile, meek, obedient, submissive
		opposites: rebellious, wild
		2 dull, lifeless, unexciting
		opposites: bold, exciting
tasteful	*adj*	artistic, delicate, elegant, graceful, refined, stylish
		opposites: inelegant, tasteless
tasty	*adj*	appetising, delicious, flavourful, mouthwatering, savoury, succulent
		opposites: disgusting, tasteless
teach	*verb*	advise, coach, discipline, drill, inform, instruct, show, train, tutor
		opposites: learn, study
tear	*verb*	1 divide, pull, rip, sever, yank
		2 bolt, charge, dash

tease	*verb*	annoy, goad, mock, needle, pester, ridicule, taunt, torment
tedious	*adj*	annoying, boring, dreary, dull, unexciting, uninteresting
tell	*verb*	announce, communicate, inform, instruct, narrate, recount, report, say, speak, state, utter
tempt	*verb*	attract, coax, entice, incite, invite, seduce *opposites:* discourage, dissuade
tender	*adj*	1 delicate, fragile, frail, vulnerable *opposites:* coarse, hard 2 affectionate, caring, considerate, gentle, loving, sensitive, sympathetic, warm, warm-hearted *opposites:* callous, severe, tough 3 aching, bruised, painful, smarting, sore
tense	*adj*	anxious, fidgety, jumpy, nervous, stressed, uptight *opposites:* calm, relaxed
terrible	*adj*	awful, dreadful, hideous, horrible, monstrous, outrageous, revolting, unpleasant, vile *opposites:* pleasant, wonderful
terrific	*adj*	amazing, awesome, breathtaking, great, magnificent, marvellous, superb, wonderful
terrified	*adj*	alarmed, frightened, horrified, panic-stricken, scared
terror	*noun*	consternation, dread, fear, panic
test	*verb*	analyse, assess, check, examine, investigate, try, verify
thankful	*adj*	appreciative, glad, grateful, pleased, relieved *opposites:* thankless, ungrateful

thick	*adj*	1	broad, deep, not thin
			opposites: thin, slim
		2	abundant, bristling, crowded, dense, numerous, packed, swarming, teeming
			opposites: scanty, sparse
		3	dim-witted, slow, stupid, thick-headed
			opposites: bright, clever, smart
thin	*adj*	1	fine, lean, light, narrow, scrawny, slender, slim
			opposites: broad, fat, thick
		2	meagre, scant, scarce, skimpy, slight, weak, watery
			opposites: dense, solid, strong
think	*verb*		believe, consider, expect, imagine, judge, reason, reflect, remember, suppose
thorough	*adj*		careful, complete, full, painstaking, perfect, total, utter
			opposites: careless, half-hearted, incomplete, partial
thought	*noun*		concept, idea, intention, judgement, meditation, notion, opinion, reflection, view
thrash	*verb*		beat, chastise, flog, lay into, spank, trounce, wallop
threaten	*verb*		bully, endanger, intimidate, menace, pressurise, terrorise, warn
throw	*verb*		fling, heave, hurl, lob, pitch, project, toss
tidy	*adj*		clean, neat, orderly, spick-and-span, trim, well-kept
			opposites: disorderly, messy, untidy
tilt	*verb*		incline, lean, slant, slope
time	*noun*		age, duration, era, interval, measure, occasion, period, span, while
timid	*adj*		afraid, bashful, fearful, nervous, shy, timorous
			opposites: assertive, bold, bossy
tiny	*adj*		insignificant, little, microscopic, minute, small, trifling

		opposites: big, immense, large
tip	*noun*	apex, end, head, peak, pinnacle, point, summit, top
		opposites: base, bottom
tired	*adj*	dead-beat, drained, exhausted, fatigued, shattered, sleepy, weary, worn out
		opposites: active, alert, lively
tolerant	*adj*	broad-minded, easygoing, kind-hearted, open-minded, patient, sympathetic
		opposites: biased, bigoted, intolerant, prejudiced
tolerate	*verb*	allow, bear, endure, permit, put up with, suffer, take, undergo
		opposites: ban, disallow, forbid
top	*noun*	apex, crest, crown, head, high point, peak, pinnacle, summit
		opposites: base, bottom
topic	*noun*	issue, matter, question, subject, subject-matter, text, theme
torment	*verb*	annoy, bother, crucify, harass, irritate, persecute, pester, tease, worry
		opposites: comfort, ease, pacify, please
torment	*noun*	agony, anguish, distress, misery, pain, suffering, trouble
		opposites: joy, pleasure
tough	*adj*	1 hard, leathery, rigid, rough, rugged, stiff, sturdy, unyielding
		opposites: fragile, pliable, soft
		2 difficult, hard, puzzling, troublesome, unlucky
		opposites: easy, not difficult
trace	*noun*	bit, dash, drop, hint, iota, spot, tinge, touch, vestige
tradition	*noun*	custom, habit, lore, ritual, way

traditional	*adj*	customary, established, long-established, usual
		opposites: innovatory, modern
tragic	*adj*	awful, disastrous, sad, sorrowful, woeful
		opposites: comic, light-hearted
train	*verb*	coach, drill, educate, exercise, instruct, prepare, teach, tutor
transform	*verb*	alter, change, reconstruct
		opposites: keep the same, preserve
trap	*noun*	ambush, pitfall, snare, trick
	verb	ambush, corner, deceive, ensnare, trick
travel	*verb*	journey, move, proceed, roam, tour, wander
		opposites: remain, stay
treachery	*noun*	betrayal, disloyalty, double-dealing, treason
		opposites: dependability, loyalty
tremble	*verb*	quake, quiver, shake, shiver, shudder, vibrate
tremendous	*adj*	amazing, awesome, enormous, extraordinary, gigantic, great, huge, immense, sensational, wonderful
		opposites: boring, dreadful, tiny
trick	*verb*	cheat, deceive, fool, hoodwink, lead on, outwit, swindle, trap
tricky	*adj*	1 crafty, cunning, devious, foxy, scheming, wily
		opposites: honest, open
		2 complicated, difficult, risky, sticky, ticklish
		opposites: easy, uncomplicated
triumph	*noun*	achievement, conquest, mastery, rejoicing, success, victory
		opposites: disaster, setback
trivial	*adj*	insignificant, little, paltry, slight, trifling, unimportant, worthless

opposites: important, significant

trouble	*noun*	1 anxiety, bother, danger, difficulty, distress, misfortune, sorrow, worry
		opposites: calm, peace
		2 attention, care, pains
true	*adj*	1 authentic, correct, exact, precise, real, right, valid
		opposites: inaccurate, false
		2 honest, loyal, sincere, trustworthy, upright
		opposites: disloyal, untrustworthy
trust	*verb*	bank on, believe, count on, depend on, rely on, swear by
		opposite: mistrust
trustworthy	*adj*	genuine, honest, reliable, true, truthful, upright
		opposites: undependable, unreliable
truth	*noun*	certainty, fact, facts, genuineness, reality, truthfulness
		opposites: falsehood, lies, untruth
try	*verb*	attempt, endeavour, strive, struggle, taste, undertake
		opposites: give in, give up, lose heart
tune	*noun*	harmony, melody, song, theme
turn	*verb*	circle, go round, pivot, revolve, roll, twist, wheel, whirl
twist	*verb*	coil, revolve, screw, turn, wind
type	*noun*	class, example, kind, sort, species, variety
tyrant	*noun*	autocrat, despot, dictator, oppressor

U

ugly	*adj*	1 hideous, not pretty, plain, unattractive, unlovely, unsightly
		opposites: beautiful, lovely, pretty
		2 evil, horrid, nasty, offensive, revolting, vile
		opposites: charming, good
unaware	*adj*	heedless, ignorant, oblivious, unknowing, unsuspecting, unsuspicious
		opposites: aware, knowing
uncertain	*adj*	ambiguous, doubtful, hesitant, indistinct, questionable, unclear, unsure, variable
		opposites: certain, sure
uncomfortable	*adj*	awkward, embarrassed, ill-fitting, painful, troubled, uneasy
		opposites: comfortable, easy
uncommon	*adj*	exceptional, extraordinary, odd, peculiar, rare, special, unusual
		opposites: common, ordinary, unexceptional
unconcerned	*adj*	cool, detached, indifferent, uncaring, unruffled, untroubled, unworried
		opposites: concerned, involved, worried
unconscious	*adj*	1 concussed, knocked out, out cold, out for the count, senseless
		opposites: awake, aware, conscious
		2 instinctive, subconscious, unintentional
		opposites: deliberate, intentional
uncouth	*adj*	awkward, clumsy, coarse, crude, ill-mannered, uncivilised, vulgar
		opposites: polite, refined
uncover	*verb*	disclose, divulge, expose, open, reveal, show, unmask
		opposites: conceal, cover, suppress

undecided	*adj*	hesitant, in two minds, tentative, uncertain, unsure, vague
		opposites: certain, decided, sure
undergo	*verb*	endure, experience, submit to, suffer, withstand
underhand	*adj*	crooked, deceitful, dishonest, shady, unscrupulous
		opposites: above board, honest, open
understand	*verb*	appreciate, comprehend, cotton on, follow, get the message, grasp, know, realise, see
		opposites: fail to appreciate, misunderstand
undesirable	*adj*	distasteful, objectionable, offensive, unacceptable, unsuitable, unwelcome
		opposites: desirable, welcome, wished for
undisturbed	*adj*	calm, composed, placid, serene, unconcerned, unperturbed, untroubled
		opposites: disturbed, upset
undo	*verb*	1 loose, loosen, open, unbutton, unfasten, unlock, untie, unwrap
		opposites: do up, fasten
		2 destroy, overturn, spoil, upset, wreck
		opposites: advance, put together
uneasy	*adj*	anxious, disturbed, nervous, restless, tense
		opposites: calm, composed
unequal	*adj*	different, ill-matched, unbalanced, uneven, unlike
		opposites: balanced, equal, matching
unequalled	*adj*	best, exceptional, second to none, supreme, unsurpassed
		opposites: ordinary, second-rate
uneven	*adj*	asymmetrical, erratic, inconsistent, irregular, jerky, odd, rough, variable
		opposites: even, regular, smooth

unexpected   *adj*   accidental, chance, fortuitous, surprising, unforeseen, unusual
opposites: expected, normal, predictable

unfair   *adj*   1 biased, bigoted, prejudiced, unsporting
opposites: even-handed, fair

2 undeserved, unjust, unmerited, wrong
opposite: deserved

unfaithful   *adj*   deceitful, false, fickle, treacherous, unreliable, untrustworthy
opposites: faithful, loyal

unfinished   *adj*   crude, imperfect, incomplete, rough, unpolished, unrefined
opposites: finished, polished, refined

unfit   *adj*   1 decrepit, feeble, unhealthy
opposites: fit, healthy

2 inadequate, ineffective, unequal, unsuitable, useless
opposites: suitable, useful

unfortunate   *adj*   1 luckless, star-crossed, unlucky, unsuccessful
opposites: fortunate, lucky, successful

2 disastrous, poor, unhappy, unsuitable, untimely, wretched
opposites: fortunate, happy, successful

unfriendly   *adj*   hostile, inhospitable, quarrelsome, surly, unapproachable, unsociable
opposites: amiable, friendly, good-natured

unhappy   *adj*   depressed, downcast, miserable, mournful, sad, sorrowful, wretched
opposites: contented, happy

uniform   *noun*   costume, dress, outfit, robes, suit

unimportant   *adj*   immaterial, insignificant, minor, negligible, paltry, slight, trivial *opposites:* important, major

unique	*adj*	one-off, only, solitary, unequalled, unprecedented, unrivalled

opposite: commonplace

unit	*noun*	component, element, item, member, part, piece, portion, section

unite	*verb*	combine, cooperate, join, join forces, link, marry, merge, unify

opposites: separate, sever

universal	*adj*	all-inclusive, all-round, common, entire, general, total, whole, widespread

opposites: particular, specific

unjust	*adj*	one-sided, prejudiced, unfair, wrong

opposites: just, right

unkind	*adj*	callous, cruel, inconsiderate, mean, spiteful, uncaring, unfriendly, unsympathetic

opposites: considerate, kind

unknown	*adj*	anonymous, concealed, hidden, mysterious, secret, strange, unfamiliar

opposites: known, understood

unlikely	*adj*	improbable, questionable, suspicious, unbelievable, unexpected, unimaginable

opposites: likely, probable

unlucky	*adj*	ill-fated, jinxed, luckless, unfortunate

opposites: fortunate, lucky

unnecessary	*adj*	needless, non-essential, superfluous, uncalled for, unneeded, useless

opposites: essential, necessary, needed

unreasonable	*adj*	1 erratic, foolish, headstrong, inconsistent, irrational
		opposites: rational, reasonable
		2 absurd, excessive, immoderate, unjust, unjustifiable, unwarranted
		opposites: due, fitting, proper
unruly	*adj*	disobedient, headstrong, lawless, rebellious, uncontrollable, unmanageable, wild, wilful
		opposites: manageable, obedient, well-behaved
unsatisfactory	*adj*	disappointing, inadequate, mediocre, poor, unacceptable, unsuitable, weak
		opposites: acceptable, good, satisfactory, suitable
unskilled	*adj*	incompetent, unskilful, untalented, untrained
		opposites: expert, skilled, trained
unsure	*adj*	doubtful, hesitant, insecure, suspicious, tentative, uncertain, undecided
		opposites: confident, determined, sure
untidy	*adj*	disorderly, jumbled, messy, rumpled, scruffy, sloppy, slovenly
		opposites: neat, tidy
untrue	*adj*	false, incorrect, misleading, untruthful, wrong
		opposites: honest, true
unusual	*adj*	abnormal, curious, extraordinary, odd, rare, remarkable, strange, uncommon, unexpected
		opposites: common, expected, normal, usual
unwise	*adj*	foolish, ill-advised, ill-judged, imprudent, indiscreet, irresponsible, rash, reckless, stupid, thoughtless
		opposites: prudent, sensible, wise
upright	*adj*	1 erect, perpendicular, straight, upstanding, vertical
		opposites: flat, horizontal
		2 good, honest, just, noble, true, trustworthy, virtuous
		opposites: devious, dishonest, ignoble

uproar	*noun*	clamour, commotion, din, noise, pandemonium, riot, ruction, turmoil
		opposites: calm, peace, quiet
upset	*verb*	1 capsize, overturn, tip, topple
		2 annoy, bother, disturb, perturb, trouble
urgent	*adj*	critical, immediate, pressing, top-priority
		opposite: non-urgent
use	*verb*	1 employ, handle, manipulate, utilise, wield
		opposites: misuse, waste
		2 consume, exhaust, spend, waste
		opposites: keep, retain
useful	*adj*	handy, helpful, practical, profitable, valuable, worthwhile
		opposites: ineffective, unhelpful, useless
useless	*adj*	fruitless, futile, hopeless, ineffective, pointless, unprofitable, worthless
		opposites: effective, helpful, useful
usual	*adj*	accepted, common, customary, expected, familiar, general, normal, ordinary, typical
		opposites: uncommon, unheard of, unusual
utter	*verb*	declare, express, pronounce, say, speak, state, tell, voice

V

vacant	*adj*	1 empty, free, to let, unfilled, unoccupied, void
		opposites: full, occupied
		2 dreamy, expressionless, inattentive, unthinking
		opposites: attentive, lively
vacuum	*noun*	emptiness, gap, nothingness, space, void
vague	*adj*	doubtful, fuzzy, hazy, indefinite, inexact, shadowy, uncertain, unclear
		opposites: certain, clear, definite
vain	*adj*	1 bigheaded, conceited, proud, self-satisfied, stuck-up
		opposites: humble, modest
		2 fruitless, futile, pointless, useless
		opposites: helpful, useful
valid	*adj*	genuine, good, legitimate, proper, sound
		opposites: invalid, not proper, unsound
valuable	*adj*	beneficial, helpful, profitable, useful, valued, worthwhile
		opposites: useless, valueless
value	*noun*	1 charge, cost, price
		2 advantage, help, importance, merit, use, worth
		opposites: disadvantage, insignificance, unimportance
vanish	*verb*	die out, disappear, dissolve, fade, melt away
		opposites: appear, materialise
vapour	*noun*	breath, damp, fog, haze, mist, smoke, steam
variety	*noun*	1 assortment, collection, difference, mixture, variation
		opposites: sameness, similarity
		2 class, kind, make, sort, type
various	*adj*	assorted, different, many, several, varied
		opposite: same

vast	*adj*	colossal, enormous, gigantic, huge, immense, tremendous, unlimited
		opposites: insignificant, minute, small, tiny
vendetta	*noun*	bad blood, blood feud, feud, quarrel, rivalry
		opposites: alliance, friendship
vengeance	*noun*	an eye for an eye, retaliation, retribution, revenge, tit for tat
		opposite: forgiveness
venom	*noun*	1 poison
		opposite: antidote
		2 hate, malice, spite, vindictiveness
		opposite: love
verbal	*adj*	oral, spoken, word-of-mouth
		opposites: not spoken, written
verdict	*noun*	conclusion, decision, judgement, opinion, sentence
verify	*verb*	check, confirm, prove, support, testify
		opposites: discredit, invalidate, prove wrong
versatile	*adj*	adaptable, flexible, handy, multi-purpose, resourceful
		opposites: inflexible, limited, rigid
vertical	*adj*	erect, on end, perpendicular, upright, upstanding
		opposites: flat, horizontal
vessel	*noun*	1 boat, craft, ship
		2 canister, container, holder, jar, pot, utensil
vibrate	*verb*	fluctuate, pulsate, quiver, shake, shiver, throb, tremble
vice	*noun*	bad habit, evil, fault, sin, weakness, wickedness
		opposites: decency, good, goodness, virtue

vicious	*adj*	cruel, dangerous, nasty, savage, vile, violent, wicked
		opposites: gentle, good, virtuous
victim	*noun*	casualty, fall guy, scapegoat, sufferer
		opposites: attacker, killer, pursuer, slayer
victory	*noun*	conquest, success, triumph
		opposites: defeat, failure, loss
view	*noun*	1 landscape, outlook, prospect, spectacle, vista
		2 attitude, belief, feeling, impression, opinion
		opposites: indifference, lack of interest
viewpoint	*noun*	angle, attitude, feeling, opinion, position, standpoint
vigilant	*adj*	alert, careful, on one's guard, watchful, wide-awake
		opposites: careless, forgetful, negligent
vigorous	*adj*	active, energetic, lively, lusty, powerful, robust, strong, virile
		opposites: feeble, lifeless, weak
vindictive	*adj*	evil, merciless, spiteful, unforgiving, vengeful
		opposites: forgiving, merciful
violent	*adj*	destructive, powerful, rough, savage, strong, uncontrollable, vicious, wild
		opposites: calm, gentle, moderate, peaceful
virile	*adj*	macho, manly, red-blooded, robust, strong
		opposite: weak
virtue	*noun*	chastity, goodness, honour, innocence, integrity, morality, purity, worthiness
		opposites: evil, sin, vice, wickedness, wrongdoing
virtuous	*adj*	good, honest, innocent, praiseworthy, pure, spotless, upright
		opposites: evil, immoral, wicked
visible	*adj*	apparent, conspicuous, evident, obvious, open, plain, seen
		opposites: hidden, invisible

vital   *adj*   critical, crucial, essential, important, necessary
opposites: inessential, unimportant

vivacious   *adj*   bubbling, high-spirited, lively, sparkling, sprightly
opposites: dull, unexciting

vivid   *adj*   bright, brilliant, clear, glowing, intense, rich, sharp, striking, vibrant
opposites: dull, lifeless

vocal   *adj*   1 oral, said, spoken, uttered, voiced
opposite: written

2 articulate, eloquent, forthright, frank, outspoken
opposites: quiet, reticent, withdrawn

void   *noun*   cavity, chasm, emptiness, gap, hollow, space, vacuum

volume   *noun*   amount, bulk, capacity, mass, size

voluntary   *adj*   free, of one's own accord, optional, unforced, unpaid
opposites: compulsory, constrained

volunteer   *verb*   offer, present, propose, put forward, suggest
opposites: decline, hold back, keep back, refuse

voracious   *adj*   greedy, hungry, insatiable, ravenous
opposite: satisfied

vote   *noun*   ballot, election, poll, referendum, show of hands

vow   *noun*   oath, pledge, promise

vulgar   *adj*   coarse, common, indelicate, low, rude, uncouth
opposites: elegant, mannerly, polite, refined

vulnerable   *adj*   defenceless, exposed, sensitive, susceptible, unprotected, weak
opposites: invincible, safe, strong

W

wager	*noun*	bet, gamble, speculation, stake
wages	*noun*	earnings, pay, remuneration, salary
wait	*verb*	delay, hold back, linger, loiter, remain, stay
		opposites: depart, go, leave
waken	*verb*	arouse, awaken, rouse, stimulate
wander	*verb*	drift, meander, ramble, roam, stray
		opposites: remain, stay
want	*verb*	crave, desire, hanker after, long for, require, wish, yearn for
warlike	*adj*	aggressive, combative, hawkish, hostile, militaristic, pugnacious, truculent
		opposites: non-violent, peaceable
warm	*adj*	1 heated, hot, lukewarm, not cold, tepid
		opposites: cold, cool
		2 affectionate, friendly, loving, pleasant, tender
		opposites: indifferent, unfriendly
warn	*verb*	advise, alert, caution, forewarn, inform, tip off
		opposites: surprise, take by surprise
wary	*adj*	(on the) alert, apprehensive, careful, cautious, guarded, on the lookout, suspicious, watchful
		opposites: careless, reckless, unwary
waste	*verb*	destroy, exhaust, fritter away, misspend, misuse, spend, squander
		opposites: look after, preserve
watch	*verb*	contemplate, gaze at, look at, note, observe, see, view
wavy	*adj*	curly, ridged, winding, zigzag
		opposites: flat, smooth, straight
way	*noun*	1 course, direction, journey, path, road, route
		2 manner, means, method, system

weak	*adj*	1 delicate, fragile, frail, puny, thin, wanting
		opposites: robust, strong
		2 cowardly, feeble, inadequate, pathetic, spineless, vulnerable, wishy-washy
		opposites: firm, forceful, powerful, strong
wealth	*noun*	abundance, assets, fortune, plenty, prosperity, riches
		opposite: poverty
wealthy	*adj*	affluent, comfortable, moneyed, opulent, prosperous, rich, well-off
		opposites: down-at-heel, poor
weary	*adj*	dead beat, dog-tired, exhausted, fatigued, tired, worn out
		opposites: excited, fresh, lively
well-known	*adj*	famous, notable, popular, renowned
		opposites: unheard of, unknown
wet	*adj*	damp, dripping, moist, soaked, soaking, watery
		opposites: arid, dry, parched
whisper	*verb*	1 breathe, hiss, murmur, sigh
		opposites: shout, speak loudly
		2 gossip, hint, insinuate
white	*adj*	bloodless, colourless, pale, silver, snowy
		opposites: black, dark
whole	*adj*	complete, entire, perfect, total, undivided
		opposites: partial, partly
wholehearted	*adj*	determined, enthusiastic, sincere, unqualified, zealous
		opposites: half-hearted, insincere, without conviction
wicked	*adj*	bad, corrupt, evil, fiendish, immoral, nasty, sinful, vicious
		opposites: decent, good, harmless, upright

wide	*adj*	broad, expanded, large, loose, outstretched, spacious
		opposites: limited, narrow
wild	*adj*	disorderly, fierce, raging, savage, undisciplined, unmanageable, unruly, untamed
		opposites: docile, orderly, tame, tamed
wilderness	*noun*	desert, jungle, wasteland
wily	*adj*	crafty, cunning, foxy, scheming, shifty, shrewd, shy, underhand
		opposites: frank, guileless, innocent, open
win	*verb*	achieve, acquire, capture, catch, conquer, earn, gain, get, secure
		opposites: fail, lose, submit, surrender
wind (rhymes with 'find')	*verb*	coil, curl, encircle, furl, loop, roll, turn, twist
		opposites: straighten out, unwind, wind back
wind (rhymes with 'tinned')	*noun*	breeze, gale, gust, hurricane
wise	*adj*	clever, intelligent, knowing, sensible, shrewd, well-informed
		opposites: foolish, irrational, silly
wit	*noun*	1 humour, levity, repartee
		opposite: seriousness
		2 intellect, judgement, sense, understanding
		opposite: stupidity
withdraw	*verb*	1 back out, draw back, fall back, pull out, retire, retreat
		opposites: advance, go in, proceed
		2 retract, take back
		opposites: assert, emphasise, reassert
witty	*adj*	amusing, clever, comic, funny, humorous
		opposites: dull, unfunny

wonder	*verb*	ask oneself, doubt, inquire, ponder, question, think
wonderful	*adj*	amazing, astonishing, great, incredible, marvellous, outstanding, remarkable, superb, tremendous *opposites:* ordinary, unremarkable
work	*noun*	1 business, employment, industry, job, livelihood, occupation, profession *opposites:* idleness, inactivity, unemployment
		2 effort, exertion, labour, slog, toil *opposites:* leisure, play
worry	*verb*	disturb, perturb, trouble, upset *opposites:* comfort, reassure
	noun	anxiety, care, concern, fear, trouble *opposites:* comfort, reassurance
worship	*verb*	adore, glorify, honour, idolise, love, pray to, revere, venerate *opposites:* despise, hate
worth	*noun*	1 cost, price, quality, value
		2 excellence, goodness, importance, use
worthless	*adj*	good-for-nothing, meaningless, useless, valueless *opposites:* valuable, worthwhile
wreck	*verb*	break, demolish, destroy, ruin, smash, spoil *opposites:* make good, repair
wrong	*adj*	1 inaccurate, incorrect, not true, untrue, wide of the mark *opposites:* correct, right, spot on
		2 bad, immoral, sinful, undesirable, unjust, wicked *opposites:* good, just, moral, virtuous

Y

yank	*verb*	haul, heave, jerk, pull, snatch, tug
yell	*verb*	bawl, bellow, howl, roar, scream, shout, shriek, squeal
		opposites: murmur, speak quietly, whisper
yellow	*adj*	flaxen, gold, golden, lemon, mustard, saffron
yield	*verb*	1 admit defeat, cave in, give in, give up, knuckle under, relinquish, submit, surrender
		opposites: conquer, defeat, stand up to, withstand
		2 give, produce
		opposites: keep back, receive, withhold
young	*adj*	adolescent, early, fledgling, immature, junior, juvenile, youthful
		opposites: aged, old
youth	*noun*	1 adolescence, immaturity, young man
		opposites: age, maturity, middle age, old age
		2 young people, younger generation
		opposites: elderly, older generation
youthful	*adj*	boyish, childish, fresh, girlish, immature, lively, sprightly, young
		opposites: aged, senile

Z

zeal	*noun*	devotion, eagerness, enthusiasm, fanaticism, fervour, fire, keenness, passion, spirit
		opposites: apathy, indifference, lack of interest
zealous	*adj*	eager, earnest, enthusiastic, fervent, keen, passionate, spirited
		opposites: apathetic, unenthusiastic
zigzag	*verb*	meander, snake, wind
		opposite: go straight
zone	*noun*	area, district, region, section, sector, sphere, territory
zoom	*verb*	dash, hurtle, race, rush, shoot, speed, streak, zip